Irish Sporting Memories

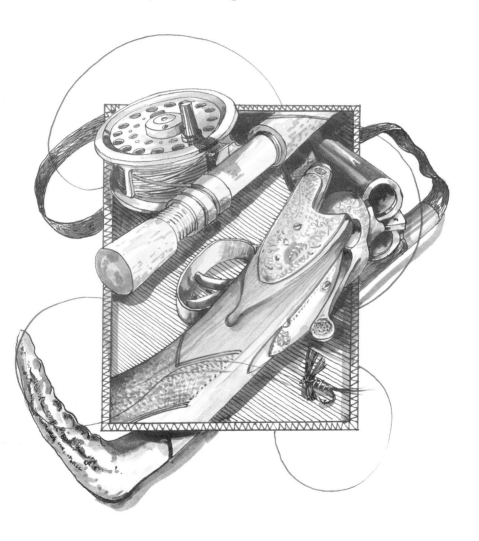

Published by
Albert J Titterington & Diana Ewings (The Author's Daughter)

Enquiries :
Country Lifestyle Exhibitions Ltd, Cranley Hill, Woodgrange Road,
Downpatrick
BT30 8JE
E: countrysportsandcountrylife@btinternet.com
ISBN No : 978-0-9558934-0-7

The late Michael & Cynthia Twist at a Trial at Enniskillen with
Ir Ch Bryanstown Shannon of Yeo & Ir Ch Bryanstown Camrose Gail

IRISH SPORTING MEMORIES

By

MICHAEL F. TWIST

Illustrations by JOHN ANKERS

Titterington & Ewings
2008

Dedication

This book is both a tribute to, and a celebration of, the life of Michael F. Twist who brought so much pleasure to country sports people through his life and writing.

Just before his death Michael Twist wrote :

"Thanks to my parents, wife, daughter and, by no means least, my son-in-law I have had a wonderful life, so don't grieve but rejoice at what we have shared together."

We can think of no finer "epitaph" to sum up a great sportsman and inveterate storyteller.

The publishers would like to thank the late Mr and Mrs Michael Twist for their permission to publish this book posthumously, the Marquess Conyingham and the late Bobby Ganly for their contributions, John Ankers for his illustrations and Eileen Newberry for her assistance with proof reading.

Contents

FOREWORD

This book is a MUST for all those who love and are dedicated to field sports. It is full of humorous anecdotes. It recalls bags, both shooting and fishing, which today must seem almost fictional but I can assure readers they were not, for, frequently, I was involved. The author has been a good friend of mine for nearly half a century.

He regularly shot and fished with my brothers and I, proving to be a true sportsman and, once he'd been in up to his waist a few times, he became as agile as the rest of us at crossing an Irish 'movey' bog, which, I can assure those who haven't tried it, is no mean feat.

The book recalls wonderful days from the past, the like of which will certainly never be seen again. Days when one could walk freely with a gun across wild and unspoilt countryside rich with snipe and duck, or fish rivers or loughs, as yet to be polluted by man's stupidity and greed. Reading Michael's book has reawakened many memories of bags not mentioned, like when on the 5th and 6th November 1955 we shot 188 snipe in a day and a half at Ballygar, or another time when we accounted for 125 on the same shoot. But this book is not about numbers, it is about sporting days spent with friends in unspoilt, wild and wonderful surroundings.

I can not vouch for the activities of Colonel Lawless, or my friend's companion whilst shooting 'cock' by Lough Corrib, but I can assure readers that Ireland is a land of mystery. Were my brother Jim and George McVeagh still alive, they would surely confirm this, for they had many an eerie and scalp-tingling experience in the latter's home in Co. Meath. I can, however, recollect so many days Michael and I spent together, like the one we shot together in Meath in torrential rain – we must have been mad! Barbours and suchlike waterproof coats were a thing of the future, but, in spite of appalling conditions, we shot forty-four head in a little over half a day. These days, over the same area, I doubt one would see even half that number in a week – never mind shoot them!

I remember vividly the day the author, my brother David, Mount (the Earl of Mount Charles) and I shot one hundred and thirty-one snipe at Banagher in a short day. Undoubtedly the last big bag of snipe shot there and probably in the country as a whole. Had there been a wind there is no telling what the tally might have been, for as Danny Moran said 'wasn't th' place crawling with snipes'. I can thoroughly recommend 'Irish Sporting Memories' as a truly enjoyable and humorous read.

Bobby Ganly

CHAPTER 1

'For a Sassenach you'll do.'

Many have dreams, but only a few realise even a small proportion of them. However, fortune smiled on me on the morning of the 5th November 1947, as I walked down the gangplank off the Liverpool to Dublin ferry, minutes after docking. I was about to take up residence as Land Agent to the 2nd Duke of Westminster in charge of his Irish estates and interests. I had made a fleeting, but whirlwind visit with George Ridley, the Duke's Chief agent, three weeks previously.

Great! I was delighted to join His Grace's staff and had been warned by Ridley that it would entail one hundred percent commitment. That in no way fazed me, for I had, on being invalided out of the army early in the war, become resident land agent, managing the Roundhill Estate in the Vale of Aylesbury, for a MFH, who was also one of the country's leading industrialists and probably the most dynamic personality I ever met. However, whilst the prospects of working for the Duke was a great incentive for moving to Ireland, there was an even greater one – the hunting, shooting and fishing for which the country was renowned.

I had grown up on an agricultural estate where my father was resident land agent. From a very early age I had become wholly involved in field sports, together with the many joys and interests of the countryside. I shot my first bolted rabbit from ferrets when a mere 7 ½ years old. I should add this was under the strictest supervision of one of the gamekeepers, Bob Hedges, employed on the estate, who had been a sergeant in the army during the first World War. Talk about 'King's Regulations'! Father's and Bob's safety regulations put them completely in the shade and, believe me, they were implemented one hundred percent plus. One deviation, however small and one was in deep, deep trouble and rightly so.

I started fly fishing when I was about nine, albeit wet fly and did not advance to savour the pleasures of working a dry fly until I was about thirteen. I have no idea when I started coarse fishing but it was certainly before shooting and something I virtually gave up once I had experienced the pleasures of fly fishing, except spinning for pike. Riding came a little later, but, once seriously into it, became my first love, although in racing parlance it would have needed a photo finish to split the three.

I became an avid reader at an early age but not the books which would normally be associated with a lad from about eight years onwards. Patrick Chalmers was much favoured. Being 'horse mad,' Charles J Payne, better known as 'Snaffles', who was considered to be on a par with Lionel Edwards when it came to sporting and country scenes, was another. A much favoured book was 'Red Letter Days' by M J Farrell and illustrated by 'Snaffles'.

Long, long before I even thought of moving to Ireland to work, it had become my ambition to visit the Emerald Isle – which over the years had developed into Utopia when applied to field sports. A conclusion greatly strengthened by Major A W Long's 'Irish Sport of Yesterday', a book high on my 're-read list'. A fascinating story of how he and a friend, just after the 1914-18 war, had taken a house in the West of Ireland where, so it seemed, snipe and woodcock abounded and the rivers were full of salmon. Others such as White's 'Selborne' and Henry Williamson's 'Tarka the Otter' graced my bedside bookcase, both, incidentally, prizes won at the Preparatory School I attended for the best essay of the year. Other authors like D Watkins Pitchford and Brian Vesey-Fitzgerald helped fill the shelves of my bookcase and my mind with dreams – dreams of snipe rising *screeching* from their watery habitat, the silver flashes as salmon leapt high as they made their way up river to spawn and the daunting banks of counties Tipperary and Limerick, over which that noted pack of foxhounds, the Scarteen, (The Black and Tans) hunted.

Since those boyhood days I'd hunted with a number of packs, albeit some of them only once, trying horses for the MFH for whom I worked. I'd enjoyed excellent shooting and memorable days fishing the rivers Torridge and Exe. Yet as I climbed into a cab to drive me to the accommodation that George McVeagh, the Duke's solicitor in Dublin, had found for me, the euphoria of those childhood dreams returned. In my fleeting visit, three weeks before, I had seen much of George considering the time I'd been in Ireland. We seemed to hit it off at once and to my delight I learned he was a keen shooting man but at the time I did not appreciate what a brilliant snipe shot he was, undoubtedly one of the all time greats. Further, he promised to introduce me to the intricacies of snipe shooting over the bogs and marshes of his native land. As he said this he had given me a sidelong glance, adding, "That is if you're tough enough to stay the course".

My cab stopped outside No. 4 Dartmouth Road, the cabbie willingly helping hump my considerable amount of luggage into what was to be my home for the next two to three years. I had a quick wash and brush up, breakfasted and headed for McVeagh's offices in Kildare Street, virtually opposite the entrance to Dail Eireann, the Irish Parliament. An hour later I collected a **new** car which George had somehow acquired for me. This was a major achievement as new cars in Ireland, as indeed in England, were rarer than the proverbial hen's teeth.

Around noon I met up with Dick Powley, who had, for several years, been head herdsman caring for the Dairy Shorthorn herd on the Roundhill Estate. Dick was born on the Duke's Eaton Estate in Cheshire and had worked there as one of the under herdsmen for a number of years, before branching out to take a senior position. He only remained a month after I left Roundhill and was delighted to be joining me in Ireland as Steward-cum-Head-Herdsman for the Duke's Dairy Shorthorns and farms at Maynooth, Co Kildare, eventually living at Derrinstown once the farmhouse had been modernised.

Derrinstown for me had two interesting non-agricultural features. Firstly, some marshy land which undoubtedly would hold snipe and, which I equally knew, in the interests of good husbandry, I would eventually have to drain. Secondly, the River Ryewater bounded one side of the property, appearing to offer excellent habitat for duck, but alas, for the moment, pressing ducal duties had to take precedence over youthful dreams. Nevertheless I was determined, at the first opportunity, to mix business with pleasure and have a gun under my arm when next I walked the Maynooth farms.

Two full days after my arrival in Ireland I set off for Lismore, Co Waterford, where the Duke's residence, Fort William, was superbly sited overlooking the River Blackwater, about a mile of which went with the property. The Blackwater was a noted salmon river, two excellent pools being included in the Fort William reach. When the Duke came to know me, he told me I could fish them any time I liked. Then with a chuckle he'd added, "But I don't expect you have a lot of time for such things with all you have to do for me". I laughed, for it was said jokingly, and replied that with such an offer I'd make time.

The next day I drove across to the stud farm at Bruree, Co Limerick, where the Duke's eldest daughter, Lady Ursula, lived with her husband Major Stephen Vernon and with whom I lunched. However, I spent the main of the day walking the property with Tom Beedleston, the stud groom, who combined his duties as such with that of Steward. When I left Tom for my luncheon appointment we only had an area known as The Garoose, some fifty acres of rushy uncared for farm land, to walk in the afternoon and discuss the possibility of draining it to once again make it productive agricultural land.

Over lunch I happened to say what I would be doing in the afternoon. On hearing this Lady Ursula said, "Oh, do tell Beedlestone to take his gun. I'm having a dinner party tomorrow night and some snipe would be an excellent addition." In due course I conveyed her ladyship's message. For a moment Tom looked slightly embarrassed, but I assured him I had no objection, we could still discuss the project that was being considered.

He smiled, then said, "Quietly, I hope". He paused, "I know you've done a lot of shooting Mr Twist, but has this included snipe shooting?" I replied that whilst it was true I'd had a lot of excellent pheasant and partridge shooting, the number of snipe I'd shot could easily be counted on the fingers of my two hands. Tom then explained two essentials for successful snipe shooting. Firstly, silence was of the essence, secondly always walk marshes and bogs, as near as possible, with the wind in one's back. He went on to explain that snipe dislike flying directly into the wind and when they do rise, just for a split second, will hang in the air giving a Gun that fraction of a second before departing, their jinking flight immediately making them a far more difficult target.

We drove to the end of the tarmacadam road, although it could be rated little more than a lane, before continuing along the gravel potholed track that ran down the side of The Garoose, continuing into the distance through wild and marshy countryside. Fortunately what we were about to walk was just badly drained agricultural land, covered with patches of tussocks of both grass and rushes. Tom assured me this would be easily negotiated in normal knee-length rubber boots. He tested for the direction of the wind, for all intents and purposes there wasn't any. Tom remarked that this could be bad as snipe, with their very sensitive hearing, might and usually did, jump well out of range under such conditions. However, just very occasionally, it could have a reverse effect. Fortunately for Lady Ursula's dinner party this was one of those days.

The snipe sat well and Tom proved to be a more than average Shot and by the time we'd finished our walk his game bag held 13 snipe and 2 teal. It was certainly the most snipe I had ever seen at one time and said so to Tom. It transpired it was also the most he had ever seen in The Garoose. He offered me the teal, but I declined, suggesting that he and his wife should have them. He thanked me, seeming genuinely pleased and told me that teal were their favourite duck.

It was dark when I left Bruree and started off on what I found to be a long and tiring drive back to Dublin, long more in time than distance. First there was some eighteen miles of pretty rugged, but reasonably straight road across to Limerick. However, there were just enough bends which I discovered, over the years, which on rounding, might occasionally produce the unexpected. I remember a bunch of cattle being driven back from a fair on a dark winter's night, a hurricane lantern or any other form of light being considered a totally unnecessary appendage – weren't cattle on the roads long before there were cars? Stray horses, frequently donkeys and a host of other obstacles, too great to list, could confront the unwary motorist.

From Limerick I set off for Dublin along a section of road which, I was to find in winter time, could be deserted for many miles, before reaching Nenagh. The next section to Roscrea was more 'motorist friendly' as one passed through several villages to Portlaoise. Tired from both work and driving roads I did not know I decided to stop at the hotel for a short break and a bite to eat, before the final leg to Kildare, across the Curragh, the home of Irish racing; then onto Naas and finally Dublin, and Dartmouth Road. When I reached my room I made a beeline to the cupboard in which there was a bottle of 12 year old Powers Gold Label Whiskey and poured myself a much needed drink.

As I went to sit down I noticed a hand addressed unstamped envelope on the centre table. It proved to be a note from Harry Kellett whose daughter, Iris, was one of the top lady show jumpers in the world. He had heard from a friend in England, also involved in show jumping, that I had moved to Ireland and that I was on the panel of judges for the British Show Jumping Association – therefore obviously I was a kindred spirit. Would I care to visit him and Iris on Sunday, see the horses and stay on for a meal? It was an invitation I certainly was not going to turn down. I phoned my acceptance early the next morning. Harry suggested I should arrive around 11.00 am. We could have a look round the horses and, if I liked to come in riding kit, I could 'throw a leg over a horse', something to which I readily agreed and would undoubtedly make my day. I hadn't ridden for over a month and missed it greatly, for when running the Roundhill Estate I often spent three or four hours every day in the saddle. There were no Land Rovers in those days to drive around estates to carry out one's duties as manager; it was a case of ride or walk.

I arrived punctually at 11 am, received a warm welcome and a mug of excellent coffee. I remarked upon the quality and was told that it was from Bewleys in Grafton Street, whose coffee was to become famous in many countries in the years to come. We sat chatting around the kitchen table, discovering we had a number of mutual friends and acquaintances. It was Iris who broke up the party and said if we were going to look at some of the horses we'd better move. We looked at Iris's jumpers first. I was particularly taken with a brown mare of hers, Starlight, who was to win many major competitions for her in the years to come. I was also very impressed with a 17 hh heavy weight hunter, Spitfire, and commented on his quality. Iris had laughed, "You know the right things to say, that's Dad's favourite hunter".

I looked the 'favourite' over again, "Has he won a lot in the show ring?"

It was Harry who replied, "No. Would you like to throw a leg over him?"

I certainly would. One of the staff put a saddle and, I noted, a double bridle on him and led him out of his loose box. Iris walked round as I was about to mount and whispered, "You're very honoured, but watch out. He's a right so-and-so and will duck out from under anyone like a flash when you're cantering on. Watch him particularly at the bottom of the paddock. I've a lot of oil drums and things there which I use for building jumps. They're just the sort of excuse he'll be looking for." With that she gave me a leg up. Having adjusted my leathers and checked the girth, I walked Spitfire forward out of the yard and into the jumping paddock. He was a superb ride. I walked and trotted him round the perimeter three or four times. Butter wouldn't melt in his mouth. Harry called out to me to canter on. No problem and it was like riding in an armchair – a real quality show horse. On Iris's suggestion I popped him over a couple of fences, which he sailed over with ease.

As I passed close to my host I received instructions, "Gallop on, really push him on around the paddock two or three times. See what he can really do."

I did as instructed. Spitfire raced past what Iris said might be his 'bogey', but no, he was as good as gold. He nearly lolled me into a sense of false security, but not quite. The next time round, at full gallop, he shot out sideways, as Iris had predicted, as quick as a flash. Expecting it I stayed with him – just! I did one more circuit, before pulling up in front of Harry and Iris, who were both grinning. The former said, "Now you know why he's never won in the show ring. I've yet to find someone who can stay with him when he does that little jink when galloping on and I'm too busy at the Royal Dublin Society Horse Show to ride him myself."

That Sunday morning ride led to my eventually showing Spitfire for Harry and being placed Reserve Champion Heavyweight Hunter at the RDS. The judges, both of whom I'd judged with and shown under in England, assured me he would have been not only Champion Heavyweight, but Supreme Champion of the Show if it had not been for a rather unsightly scar on his off fore fetlock joint caused by getting tangled up in a loose strand of barbed wire, not in a fence, but left lying in some rough grass in the middle of a field, when Harry was riding him with The Ward Staghounds. It was nearly 10.00 pm when I left the Kelletts, having had a most enjoyable day, made two new friends and received the promise of a mount for the first Saturday I could manage to join them for a day with The Ward.

I had got into the habit of dropping in at the Shelbourne Rooms for a quick drink or two before going back to Dartmouth Road for dinner. George McVeagh frequently did the same and had introduced me to a number of both charming and knowledgeable people, including his good friend Jim Ganly. Like George, Jim was an all round sportsman and apart from gaining eleven caps playing rugby football for his country, he also represented it at cricket and even more interesting from my point of view, was a keen fisherman and an excellent shot. Further, I was to learn that he and George were regular shooting companions.

An evening or two after visiting the Kelletts I dropped in at The Rooms. Both George and Jim were sitting up at the bar and beckoned me over to join them. I was on my second Powers when George casually asked me if I'd be interested in joining the two of them the coming Sunday to shoot snipe in Co Meath. Thinking about it now I must have sounded almost hysterical with excitement. At last the start of the dream was going to be realised. Suddenly an awful thought crossed my mind, George had said Sunday! One didn't shoot on Sunday – it was against the law. This was a leg-pull and I voiced my fears to my companions, both of whom laughed and assured me that whilst that might well be the law in England it certainly was not the case in Ireland. I enquired where I could buy waders and cartridges? Both looked at me with obvious surprise and amusement. Jim then explained they didn't wear waders, the distance walked was such that it would make it completely impractical and, also, very tiring.

He went on to tell me that what I needed was a pair of Dunlop spiked rubber golf shoes, an old pair of trousers, preferably tucked into an equally old pair of knee length socks and one just walked in and got wet. A change of clothes was a must, for as soon as they finished shooting they went somewhere to change out of their wet clothing. George, with a sly grin, remarked that in late December and January it was a pastime that sorted the men from the boys. At that moment Bobby and David Ganly, Jim's two youngest brothers joined us, to be followed by Willie a few minutes later, who came next to Jim out of the six brothers, but only the four present were keen on fishing and shooting.

In Ireland in those days it didn't take much to start a party, it probably doesn't now, but one quickly developed that evening. I phoned Dartmouth Road to say I wouldn't be back for dinner. Around nine o'clock I was introduced to the Dolphin Hotel, noted for superb steaks and massive grilled Dover Soles. A great feature being that you could choose the one you wanted from a wide selection in a display case in front of a large and glowing charcoal grill and instruct the chef as to how you wished it cooked. There was nothing pretentious about the Dolphin Grill Room, spotlessly clean, excellent fare and matching service, patronised by a variety from every strata of Irish life. I was introduced to the owner, Jack Nugent, an amazing character and, so he claimed, a practising Catholic, who, according to him, gave up drink for Lent. However, I was to learn that Jack didn't count the best part of a bottle of sherry at lunch and another in the evening as drink – as far as he was concerned only 'the hard stuff' (spirits) could be classed as drink.

In the years that followed I spent many evenings at the Dolphin, some very memorable. One that comes to mind was dinner with a past and very famous Master of the County Galway Foxhounds, better known as the 'Blazers', Isaac Bell and the authoress Molly Keen, who wrote so many enchanting books about Ireland. Molly, for 'starters' decided to have two snipe, frequently available during the shooting season. She gave her instructions to the chef before returning to our table. When Jimmy, the headwaiter who had great Irish brogue, set them before her he said, "Begob mam, you should o' let t'em fly over th' grill twice so you should, t'ems barely stopped kicking."

He was not far wrong, when she cut into them they were as near raw as made no difference. I remember she followed them with steak tartare!

Another evening, some years later, I was having a quiet meal with my wife, then my fiancée, when a rowdy trio entered and were shown to the only vacant table, which was nearby. I realised the cause of the hubbub was the playwright Brendan Behan, who had gained a reputation as a heavy drinker and his language was far from acceptable in places like the Dolphin. His language was nothing short of disgusting and I felt something had to be done, when I saw a lady at the adjoining table pick up a large jug of water which she proceeded to empty over the playwright. Soaked and cursing loudly he left. Normally the Dolphin was full of cheerful friendly people, largely country folk, trainers and sportsmen in general, and in the twenty plus years that I was a regular I never witnessed another episode like the baptism of Behan!

On the Sunday morning I breakfasted early and arrived at George McVeagh's just before 8.00 am. Jim was already there and within minutes we were heading out of Dublin and on into deserted countryside. We'd been going for about half an hour when Jim, who was driving suddenly pulled the car to the side of the road and said 'Goldies!'

George wound down the window and there, in a field of some twenty acres or so, were many hundreds of golden plover. I'd only ever seen about a dozen in my life! A plan of campaign was quickly hatched. Jim would go up the hedge to the left. George would stay on the main road near the car and I was to go along the road to the house at the corner of the field and up the lane just beyond it. Some twenty yards past the house, my friends assured me, was a favourite line frequently taken by the plover. I had considerable misgivings about shooting on a Sunday, walking down the road with a loaded gun, George had said I should load – just in case, and of taking up my position so close to a house.

Subconsciously, as I passed, it struck me that the house was rather superior compared with others I had seen adjoining the road as we had driven out from the city. Before I could give it further thought there were two quick shots from the far side of the field. The sky looked black with plover and it seemed all heading towards me. I pressed tighter to the hedge, remembering the advice Jim had given. "Don't brown them, pick a bird and the chances are you'll get two or three.'

As the first of the flock crossed the line of the hedge I stood up, swing on a bird and pulled on the trigger. I saw three start to fall as I lined up another, virtually over the house – two more. I reloaded and got off both barrels before they were gone, adding two more to my tally. I heard Jim and George firing and then all was quiet.

I clambered over the hedge and picked up six, but nowhere could I see the seventh. I had been told not to hang around and so, reluctantly; I headed back towards the car. As I was passing the house I heard someone call out. "Would this be yours sorr?"

I glanced in the direct of the voice and there standing in the doorway was a Sergeant of the Gardai! The house was the local barracks. My heart sank into my boots. Inwardly I cursed my new friends for landing me in what was obviously going to be a lot of trouble. Smiling the sergeant walked down the path and handed me the plover I had been looking for. "Thems great eating so they are. I of'en have two or t'ree for me tay. Good luck to you sorr."

So saying he turned and retraced his steps. I stammered my thanks and continued on my way. Both Jim and George had several plover and were highly amused at my encounter with the sergeant. They just could not understand why I seemed so worried!

We arrived at the first marsh which I was to learn later was quite large for Co. Meath. As we crossed the grass field leading to it, my friends again stressed the importance of keeping moving as, in a number of places, it was bottomless once one broke through the top covering. As we neared the marsh, Jim put his finger to his lips. Quiet I had been told, was essential. Snipe were very susceptible to noise. George touched my arm and, in a whisper asked if I had a cap in my pocket that I could use. Equally quietly, I enquired why.

"Just so we know where to drop a wreath should you go through!"

I was not reassured. We lined out. I was in the middle. A wave from Jim and we moved forward. As I took my first step into the cold wet mud I felt as though my leg was going down for ever – I still had one foot on dry land. I nearly panicked and drew back but, just in time, there was a shot from George, who had already advanced some ten yards. The first snipe was in the bag.

I gritted my teeth and floundered forward. A snipe leapt, squawking just in front of me. I didn't even get the gun up; I was too busy thinking how bottomless my friends meant by bottomless. My companions waited for me to catch up as I almost wallowed through this marsh – it was just like walking on a trampoline oozing mud and water! Another snipe jumped just in front of me. I missed it, as I did the next two and the next. We were nearing the centre and the terrain seemed slightly firmer. Suddenly the place was alive with snipe. I swung on one, pulled the trigger and, to my delight, it fell. I switched to a second and that too was down. I picked the first quite easily, I had a good mark on it, but no way could I find the second. Jim came over with his Labrador bitch and within seconds he tossed the bird across to me – my first right and left of Irish snipe! When we returned to the car the bag was sixteen, of which I was proud to claim three. My companions, I noticed, missed very little.

We drove on about half a mile, Jim stopped to let George and me out. I gathered that he and I were about to set off on a walk of some five or six miles and was told to bring plenty of cartridges. Jim was going off in the car to shoot what were described as 'handy little holes'. Quickly we reached the first marsh. Much to my relief George whispered that I could walk along the edge, whilst he went through it. He seemed to flit over the moving layer of moss and rushes. I noticed he was not wet above the knees, whereas I was soaked to well up my thighs. George shot another right and left, as three snipe came my way. I got one, but hopelessly missed the second. We continued across country at a marathon pace. George seemed to know every little wet place, as well as all the marshes. Several times he deviated from our course to small patches of rushes, often not more than a few square yards; nearly every time they produced a snipe.

As we progressed my confidence increased. I began to cross the decaying vegetation and mud with less trepidation, which was reflected in my shooting. We passed through several small farmyards. Each time George went to the cottage and had a chat. At one the owner said he would accompany us to his marsh. George shot two consecutive right and lefts and as we returned to dry land the grinning owner remarked to me "Isn't Mr. Mac the master man at the snipes?"

With that he left us and we continued on our way. Several marshes further on, we were just coming out of it when a hare darted out and headed up across the field to my right. An easy shot. I put up my gun and swung on it. As I did so there was a roar from George, "No!" – He was just in time.

He came across to me. "Never, never shoot a hare." I enquired why. George explained that a large number of small farmers had one or two greyhound brood bitches and they relied on the sale of puppies to help augment their meagre incomes. Hares were greatly prized for training the saplings.

Then with a smile "Anyway, do you really want to hump a ruddy great hare for another couple of miles through bogs?" It was either 1948 or 1949 that the country's revenue from the export of greyhounds exceeded that derived from Guinness!

We continued on our way, George shooting with an ease and brilliance that I have never seen surpassed at snipe. As we were crossing a grass field and I was quietly marvelling at my friend's lightning reflexes, a teal appeared from nowhere, high overhead, but shootable. George missed with both barrels. My satisfaction was great as it collapsed to my first shot and earned a word of commendation from my companion. At last we came to a small river and followed this to a bridge. Jim was already there. He apparently had had good shooting, including a right and left of teal. As we sat on the parapet, in the autumn sunshine, I marvelled at the peace and quiet, the pureness of the air and the beauty of the countryside. We devoured our sandwiches in near silence. I for one was ravenous. I looked around me and enquired of my friends if they owned the shooting rights of all the marshes we had shot that morning. Both laughed but it was Jim who answered my query.

"Good heavens no. No one minds you shooting snipe, well hardly anyone. Nor do they mind you shooting duck. The one thing you mustn't shoot are hares. If we can, we call at the farms at the beginning of the season for a bit of a chat and, for politeness' sake, ask if it is alright to shoot the marshes. We've never been refused yet."

Soon we were off again. Whilst it was a lovely day, it wasn't that warm and, being wet nearly up to my waist, I was beginning to feel decidedly cool! The afternoon proved to be as exciting and enjoyable as the morning. We came across another flock of golden plover but were not so successful as earlier. However, Jim added two more to the bag. I was growing in confidence all the while and so was able to concentrate more on shooting and less on survival, although I was unable to emulate my friends. They seemed to know instinctively where to step, even without looking, whereas I just blundered in and out but it was undoubtedly the most exhilarating thing I had ever done. As the sun began to sink, so it became colder, but I hardly noticed. I did, however, realise that in about another twenty minutes to half an hour the light would have gone and that would see the end of the days' activities. Jim stopped the car at the end of a boreen and he and George got out. After a brief confab, George beckoned to me.

I was to go off and shoot a small marsh on my own, whilst Jim and George shot a larger one on the opposite side of the road from where the car was parked. I was given very explicit instructions as to its whereabouts. Up the lane, turn in the second gateway and it was at the bottom of the field. I would know I was right as two fields beyond I would see a large Georgian house. As I set off George called after me. "By the way the owner of the house may come out and wave to you. He's a friendly old boy, but don't pay any attention. Just keep on shooting. Oh yes, if he signals you to join him, pretend you didn't see. He'd keep you talking for hours and its getting cold."

I found my destination with ease. It was quite small as I had been told and there, two fields away was the big house. It looked a really beautiful home. Being sure I had the wind in my back, I proceeded quietly to the edge of the little marsh. Just as I reached it a mallard rose from a patch of tall reeds in the centre, followed quickly by a second. I downed them both. As I did so a dozen or more snipe rose screeching all around me, but there was no time to reload. I had great difficulty in retrieving my two duck. It was certainly the boggiest bog I had met! By the time I had them safely on dry land I was literally wet up to my armpits. I was picking up my gun, that I had left on terra firma, vowing that I must get a dog, when I heard shouting.

I looked towards the house and there, just entering the further field, was a man waving his arms frantically. I too gave a cheerful wave and headed off towards the boreen. It was getting distinctly cold. I decided to run to warm up a bit. The shouting continued, as I reached the lane hedge I turned and waved again. I jogged smartly down the track to the car. I found Jim and George already in it, engine running and heater on full blast. I climbed in and we were off.

"Did you see the Colonel?" enquired George.

"I saw someone, but remembered what you said and just waved, held up the duck and headed back here."

It wasn't long before we were in a small country town and pulled up outside a pub. Although it was 4.30pm of a Sunday afternoon it was quite obviously open. At my insistence we did a quick count of the bag. Seventy three head, made up of 54 snipe, 14 golden plover, 3 teal and 2 mallard, truly a magnificent days sport. We took our holdalls containing our dry clothes out of the boot and went in. My companions were obviously well known and received a great welcome. I was introduced to the owner and saw his amused look as he eyed my wet and bedraggled state. After a 'large one' each we went upstairs to the bathroom to change. When we returned to the bar there was a pot of tea awaiting us, described by mine host as 'blocky stuff' and a great plate of barmbrack. This we soon disposed of and, after barely a decent interval, I called for a round of drinks; not only for us, but for the three or four locals as well, all of whom seemed to know both Jim and George.

As these were being poured, who should walk in but the sergeant who had so thoughtfully given me my golden plover earlier in the day. It was obvious he knew my friends as well and accepted my offer of a drink with alacrity. He raised his glass.

"Good luck now gentlemen an' did you have a good day?"

"Absolutely wonderful, I've never had shooting like it and to finish with a right and left of mallard just made my day." I replied.

"It would, it would," said the sergeant sagely nodding his head.

"Strange thing, I had ole Colonel Lampard on th' phone a while back. Spluttering terrible he was. On about someone poaching his marsh. Quare how a man can get so worked up over a few snipes and duck that are free to come an' go as they like."

The sergeant took a good swig at his porter and turned to Jim and George. "Neither of you gentlemen could have strayed into the Colonel's marsh by mistake, so to speak?"

George looked at the sergeant straight in the eye. "You know better than that sergeant. Doesn't the whole of County Meath know the old Colonel's pixillated over his bit of bog."

"That is so, that is so," said the sergeant looking at his empty glass.

Jim ordered another round. "Must have been some foreigner, who'd know no better," continued George. "Terrible ignorant some of them."

"True, true. I'll tell you the Colonel was very wrathful so he was. Said the varmit kept waving and then ran off to the boreen an' held up a couple of duck so he did."

I felt the colour rising in my cheeks. I downed my third large Powers in one. The sergeant turned and looked at me and then at my empty glass. He gave me a definite wink and said, "I must away. Good night gentlemen."

He'd hardly closed the door before George began to laugh. Jim too. They laughed until the tears were running down their cheeks. George pressed another Powers into my hand. "For a Sassenach you'll do!" and so began more than two decades of wonderful friendship and the participation in shooting the like of which will never be seen again.

CHAPTER 2

'Is it the trouble you have Father?'

To say that my days were full the first few weeks I was in the Republic of Ireland would be an understatement. However, I was for all intents and purposes my own boss. This enabled me to take the gun when going round the farms at Maynooth and I quickly discovered some nearby marshes. After some enquiries I found the owners and was told to "bang away" – it was true, no one bothered about snipe! Further I had not been slow in taking up Harry Kellett's invitation to ride. I was anxious to keep fit, for I had heard from my ex boss, offering me a mount for the Boxing Day meet. I was going home for three days at Christmas and it would be a great opportunity to see a number of my friends.

However, Christmas was proving a problem for I had a shopping list as long as my arm. Meat, so strictly rationed in Britain, was readily available in Ireland, as was whisky. I could have filled a wheelbarrow with these items alone! Steaks were no problem, but whisky was another matter. One had to go through customs when leaving ROI, as well as when entering it and whilst easily available, if one had the right contacts, to get Scotch Whisky out of the country was another matter. It's export, having already been imported, was not allowed. The Duke expressed a desire for six bottles, the Chief Agent for three and I wanted at least that number to take to my father, but how? Strange though it may seem, I found the answer in the hunting field, but at the time did not realise my good fortune.

Harry Kellett offered me a mount for the first Saturday in December with the Ward Union. The meet was at Ratoath and it was with a certain sense of unease that I clambered onto my horse. He was a plain fiddle headed chestnut, standing about 16.3 hh, not short of scars and bumps on his legs. Harry assured me that whilst no beauty he had 'one hell of a lep in him'. As I jogged down the road in the general melee of riders, all anxious to be in front, I had certain misgivings and a definite sinking feeling in my stomach that I had never experienced before when going hunting. I thought of the previous Saturday, when I had followed in the car and had seen six riders walking their horses along in a ditch looking for a way out! The tops of their headgear could just be seen bobbing along, virtually level with the ground! Nor had I been cheered by the sight of two brawny sons of Ireland, who had arrived at the meet, just as we were moving off. Slung over their shoulders were coils of stout rope and each had a spade tied to the bar of his bike.

As I passed one gave a toothy grin and said. "If you go in deep sorr, we'll have you out in no time, so we will. Ten bob's the price an' isn't that cheap for maybe saving a life?"

I hadn't answered, but I couldn't help wondering why the remark had been addressed to me. Did I look that vulnerable? As we turned into a field off the road my mount received a hefty bump from the rear. I turned sharply, there trying to control a very fractious horse, was a young priest. I looked at his mount, a shaggy creature, more draught horse than hunter. Two things were patently obvious. Firstly the rider had little or no control and secondly the language was hardly that which one would expect from a man of the cloth. As the priest burst past, he shouted an apology as his mount set its jaw and was off at a gallop, narrowly missing hounds.

We trotted across a couple of fields. Fortunately there was a bridge for the likes of me, although I saw a number putting their horses over the yawning ditch as though it was a cavaletti. Hounds ranged out before us and suddenly one gave a whimper. The whimper became a chorus and within seconds the pack was screaming away, the huntsman doubling on his horn as he galloped after hounds. Such music could not fail to strengthen even the most faint hearted! I crammed down my hat, shortened my reins and was off. I kept a bit to the right of the main field. The first gaping ditch loomed ahead. I thought of the old adage about throwing one's heart over first, the rest would follow! My mount, who had the uninspired name of Ginger, went full gallop to the brink, braked, nearly sending me over on my own and hurled himself into space. He cleared the obstacle with feet to spare. As I gathered up my reins, a horse landed slithering beside me. It was the priest, his face alight with joy, he gave me a great grin. "He's an ignorant pig, as green as the grass he eats, but he's one hell of a pop in him for a three year old."

We galloped on together, clear of the rest of the field. Ginger sailed over chasm after chasm with an ease and surefootedness born of years of experience. With great enthusiasm and much cursing the priest stayed with us. I heard a shout from just behind me. "Swing right, swing right, the drain ahead is a terrible grave so it is."

We deviated from our straight line, circumnavigating 'the grave'. On we went over wonderful country, no wire and virtually all grass. I was really enjoying myself.

Hounds had been running hard for about forty minutes without hardly a check, when the inevitable happened. Ginger had just cleared with ease a positive arm of the sea, when I heard a flood of profanities behind me. I looked round and there was the priest picking himself off the ground, still clutching the reins as his horse slid slowly into the ditch. I pulled up and trotted back and enquired if I could help. I jumped off and loosened Ginger's girth. "What the divil can we do? Isn't this one of the biggest ditches in Co, Meath."

I didn't know the country well enough to either confirm or deny this, but I did realise we had a problem. The three year old was truly blown. To extricate him was going to be no small task, but at least he was upright. His front hooves resting just below the top of the bank, his head between them, rather as though he was begging. The mud bespattered priest looked at me. "Get on with you, I'll be alright. Don't loose a good hunt because of me."

"No. I've had quite enough and I certainly wouldn't leave you in this predicament."

"Ay but you're a Christian." Then with a grin he added. "Even if you're a bloody Sassenach. Here, hang onto the reins an' don't let him slip; somehow I must loosen his girth."

The latter proved to be a hair raising manoeuvre, with me holding the reins with one hand and grasping my hunting crop with the other, whilst the priest clung to the thong as he eased himself over the edge. After much puffing and cursing he achieved his objective and was back on dry land. Now what were we to do? I glanced across the field to our right and there, heading towards us, ropes slung over their shoulders, spades in hand, were the two men who had spoken to me at the meet.

"Is it the trouble you have father? Be the hokey we'll have him out o' there in no time at all, so we will. Don't let him slide father, he's aisy as he is, but on his side in the bottom o' the dyke he'll be a bugger – excuse the language father."

I thought this latter remark really unnecessary in view of what I had heard when the current predicament of the priestly conveyance had been narrowly avoided earlier in the hunt. With an assurance gained through great experience the 'Wreckers', as such helpful gentlemen were dubbed by that wonderful artist 'Snaffles' had two ropes around the hindquarters of the unfortunate horse in no time at all. Several other foot followers had arrived and stood giving much advice to the main participants.

Having adjusted the ropes to his satisfaction, the spokesman turned to the priest. "Right you be, now we're ready. Ten bob each is the fee father."

I cut in "At the meet you said ten bob. Nothing about each of you being paid that amount."

The ringleader eyed me up and down. "I'm thinkin' you'd be a foreigner so you would, with your quare accent an' no understanding. Ten bob each it is father. There's more in need if you's objecting."

The priest looked at me and grimaced. "The trouble is I've no money on me."

I put my hand in my breeches pocket and produced two ten shilling notes. "I'll lend it to you." I felt it was a gift for I was unlikely to see him again, but I had enjoyed the company of the sporting cleric on his shaggy unschooled ride. Anyway, there was an ulterior motive; I wanted a guide back to Ratoath.

'The Wreckers' grinning wickedly, pocketed the money and press-ganged the spectators into action hauling on the ropes. In minutes my companion's quivering nag was on dry land.

"I'm obliged to you men." And turning to me "And you too friend." The two men touched their forelocks and were gone, looking for the next unfortunately who would be requiring their services.

I felt it time I introduced myself to the reverend father. He stretched out a muddy hand. "Faith, and it's a good Samaritan you are. I'm indebted to you. The name's O'Flynn from Co. Tipperary – Patrick O'Flynn."

We walked our horses out to the road. Father Patrick tightened the girth and swung up into the saddle. I did the same.

"Be Jasus, I nearly forgot." My companion put his hand into the pocket of his faded hunting coat and produced a flask. He unscrewed the top, raised it towards me. "Sláinte." He took a good swig. "Great stuff." He passed me the flask. I took a sip. The next thing I was choking and spluttering.

When I'd got my breath back I enquired. "What in heaven's name is that?" Father Patrick laughed. "Poteen. The real thing, t'is all of three years old. I get it from me cousin in Co. Galway."

We jogged on towards Ratoath. Father Pat, as he said he liked to be called, obviously knew his way around the Meath countryside. It appeared that he was attached to a well known London presbytery, had been attending a course at the Maynooth Catholic College and was having a day with the Ward before joining his family for a short holiday in Co. Tipperary. He had an uncle who had a small farm close to Ratoath and who always ran on a few young horses; ostensibly to show and sell at the Dublin Horse Show in August. It transpired that my companion's 'da' also kept a few young horses on his farm just outside Cashel. Father Pat told me he had ridden since he could remember and had as a boy but one ambition – to be a jump jockey. However, weight had foiled his plans and to the great joy of his mother and the rest of the family, which included five brothers and four sisters, he had entered the priesthood.

We arrived back at the meet. I handed Ginger over to the groom waiting with the Kellett's horse box and tipped him liberally. I turned to say goodbye to my new friend, got in the car and headed back to Dublin. It had been a memorable afternoon. I smiled wryly as I thought of 'The Wreckers'. A couple of right villains, but with a natural charm and obvious aptitude, to make a few bob on the side.

When I got back to Dartmouth Road I entered through the back door, jacked off my hunting boots, hung up my mud-spattered coat and made my way to my room. As I passed the bathroom I turned on the hot tap. A good soak and a whiskey would, I felt, be a fitting end to a quite terrific, even if at times terrifying, afternoon! I had just become comfortably submerged, sipping my drink and mentally riding every fence again, when there was a bang on the door. Would I telephone Mr McVeagh as soon as possible – urgent.

Inwardly cursing and equally wondering what could be so important late on a Saturday afternoon, I grudgingly left the comfort of my bath, towelled quickly, donned my dressing gown, collected a shilling from my room and made my way to the pay-phone in the hall. George quickly explained the urgency. Would I like to join him, Jim and Bobby to shoot the next day at Banagher down on the Shannon? I hesitated. I had to be at Lismore on Tuesday, Bruree the next day, cross to Liverpool on Thursday night for a meeting on Friday and back that night, so that I would be in Dublin when His Grace arrived Saturday morning off the Holyhead ferry. A full week, but the answer had to be yes. It was something just over a two hour drive from Dublin to Banagher in Jim's big American car. I shared the back seat with three Labradors, whilst my companions occupied the front. I was warned that the hotel, The Shannon View, situated about eighty to one hundred yards from the river, was not of the best. Now I understand it is a most comfortable and well-run establishment, but in 1947 – well ' not of the best' was a major understatement. However, it was clean, the beds unbelievably uncomfortable, the plumbing, what there was of it, could only be described as abysmal and the food as unimaginative as it was tasteless. I was to learn in due course that it was a most excellent establishment from our point of view. Its fame was such that it deterred nearly all other would-be shooters from sampling its hospitality. Over the years, this suited us admirably for the shooting around Banagher, all free, could only be described, up to the early sixties, as fantastic.

We arrived soon after 8.30 p.m. Mrs Sullivan, wife of mine host, told us our room numbers. Jim and George always shared No.2, a barrack of a room, sparsely furnished with two old iron beds, an ancient wardrobe, two chairs and a washstand with a bowl and pitcher of water. Hot water was something one did not look for at the Shannon View when taking one's morning ablutions. Although there are exceptions to every rule. For one brief moment in time it sounded as though the hotel was 'going up market'. When Jim 'phoned to book our rooms, he was proudly told that they now employed a 'boots' who would help with the luggage when we arrived. It so happened that on this trip we were accompanied by a Papal Count, a keen shooting man.

On our arrival the 'boots' appeared. He must have been all of seventy years old! Going up the stairs one could almost hear him creak. Certainly there was no difficulty in hearing him grumble. He cheered up considerably when we each gave him two shillings and told us his name was Paddy and anything we wanted 'just let a roar'. That night as we were heading for bed, having installed a good thermal-lining in the bar, for it was a cold night, the Count nearly caused a major hiatus in the easy going administration of the hotel. He demanded that he should be brought a can of hot water in the morning. This was too much for Paddy, who went off to consult 'the boss'. In due course the former returned and, grudgingly assured the Count that hot water would be forthcoming. Surprisingly it was. The following morning, Sunday, as we were getting up we heard shouts from the Count for Paddy.

The latter eventually arrived on the landing.

"Where's my hot water?"

"Hot water is it an' didn't I bring you hot water yesterday? Who would be wanting hot water two mornings running?" With that Paddy stomped off. Nothing the Count could do would make Paddy change his mind. Soon after this the hotel returned to normality; as Rose, the maid said, "We'd enough of the grandeur!"

To return to No. 2. The bed furthest from the door was normally occupied by George. It must have been a strong contender for the title of most uncomfortable bed in Europe. Some years after my initial visit, one evening I went upstairs ahead of Jim and George. What motivated me to do what I did I have no idea. I took a large handful of twelve bore cartridges out of the pocket of my shooting coat and threw them in under the bottom sheet of George's bed. I propped myself against the doorframe to await results. Seconds later Jim and George appeared at the top of the stairs. As far as George was concerned, going to bed at Banagher could be described as an on-going process. He started to discard his clothes the moment he entered the room and continued to do so until he reached his bed. He would then pull on his pyjamas and clamber in. This particular evening had been no exception. He gave a couple of wriggles, remarked that the beds were getting worse and was asleep before I had said good night to Jim!

After we had dumped our gear we went down to the bar. There, for the first time I met Danny and Bill. The former had for years been general factotum to George and the Ganlys when shooting at Banagher. He was a 'broth of a boy' and no mistake. I would not have liked to tangle with him in his prime. He worked at the local corn mill and had a smallholding just outside the town. Bill, a diminutive little man, acted as driver. His was a most important job for, having dropped us off, he would take the car to the far end of the bog we were walking and wait for us. I was introduced and warmly welcomed. As the newcomer I did the honours.

The bar was snug, the ceiling black from turf smoke, but it had a certain character and charm, probably derived from the general bonhomie of the occupants rather than from anything else. I perched on a stool and listened to tales of past achievements – it was in fact a case of 'do you remember?' We were just finishing our second drink, when Rose put her head around the corner of the door and announced "The food is on the table so it is."

As we walked through to the dining room Jim told me that the meal would consist of brown Windsor soup, a fat mutton chop, boiled potatoes in their jackets and watery cabbage. This would be followed by a choice of jelly or Three Counties cheese and biscuits together with a pot of tea so strong you could stand a spoon up in it! He was right on all counts but it hadn't really been that difficult for, in due course, I found it never varied. When we had finished we returned to the bar. My companions, when they had arranged about the morning with Danny, were off to see a friend who lived the other end of the town. I was invited along but declined. My afternoon's exertions were beginning to catch up with me.

I bought Danny another pint of porter and a small Powers for myself. Danny, whose face was now flushed from the exertions of his elbow, needed little encouragement to recall past shoots at Banagher. "Did Mr. Mac and Mr. Jim ever tell you of the time they came down on the train just at the end of the War?"

"No."

"Well the golden plover were here in millions an' that's the truth. I never saw the like. I wires them so I do and down they come on th' train." So the story unfolded. It appeared that with great difficulty my friends had obtained cartridges and made the journey by train. Even that in itself was something of an adventure. Because coal was non-existent, the engine was fuelled with wood and keeping a good head of steam was no small achievement.

They arrived on Friday evening, to be met by Danny, the bearer of bad tidings. He had been out round all the callows, including those some four miles away adjoining the River Brosna, a tributary of the Shannon. He had seen one small flock of plover. However, my friends had shot snipe all day Saturday with great success. They continued in pursuit of their favourite quarry on Sunday morning and planned to catch the 3.20 p.m. back to Dublin. After an early lunch they headed for the Town Callow, a matter of a few hundred yards from the hotel on the far side of the river, for a final hours shooting. By then it was blowing a near gale force wind and golden plover seemed to be everywhere. Further, they were flying a line about fifty yards from the river and were 'cutting' by some convenient cover in which to hide. 'Cutting' is suddenly hurtling down towards the ground, flattening out only feet from it, flying at this height for a short distance before climbing steeply. Why they do this I have never really understood but it makes for the most exciting shooting and strangely, flock after flock will always 'cut' in the same place when they are flying a line. Find that place and you are in business. That's just what George and Jim did that Sunday afternoon.

Danny took another swallow. His glass was empty. When refilled he continued, "Well, I could see I'd be needing at least a couple of sacks for all the birds so I tells Mr Jim I were going back to fetch some. 'Go to the station,' says he, 'an' get them to hold the train. Take them a few bottles of beer.' I'm telling you, when I called on my way to the hotel, Liam, he's yer man at th' station, was none too pleased."

Danny continued to tell me that not having been told exactly how much beer to take, he decided on a crate of two dozen stout (Guinness). This he delivered, had a couple with Liam who agreed, after the second one, to hold the train for an hour. But what about the passengers? There wouldn't be a lot on a Sunday afternoon, but as station master-cum-porter he felt they had to be considered. Danny went back to the hotel for another crate! The station was only about two hundred yards across the river from where my two friends were having such sport. Danny told me he saw the train pull in about twenty minutes late. Soon a small gathering of some eight or ten people were congregated at the end of the platform to watch the shooting. Jim and George continued to shoot until they had run out of cartridges, which was around four o'clock. It had gone 4.30 pm before they had been back to the hotel, changed and made their way to the station, accompanied by Danny carrying two sacks of plover and snipe. They were greeted with great enthusiasm and Liam solemnly invited them to 'have a jar' with himself, the driver, the stoker and guard before they left. According to Danny they were eventually away just after 5.00 p.m.

"I'm telling you that were no slow train to Dublin! Stop at every station it should have. Be the hokey, I heard tell it burst through

Ballycumber and Clara the whistle screechin' an' sparks flying out of the stack so there was and didn't stop until it reached Kilcock, not that short o' Dublin."

"Wasn't there a terrible row over it?"

"For why? Didn't everyone have a grand afternoon and all, except the widow Mulligan, was bound for Dublin anyway. She, the poor crature, was going to a wake at Ballycumber, just six or seven miles up the line. Didn't she have a great ride and they flagged th' next down train an' she were there in plenty of time for the jollifications so she was."

I offered Danny another pint, but he declined saying he must away for hadn't we a busy day ahead of us tomorrow. I made my way up the stairs for my first night of many to be spent at the Shannon View. In spite of the fact that the mattress was all lumps and bumps I slept like the proverbial log.

The next day was cloudy with a strong wind. I shot with George which was an exhilarating and tiring experience. He was like a Jack Snipe flitting from one wet spot to another and seemed to have boundless energy. I acquitted myself reasonably well on a day that surpassed my wildest dreams and expectations of shooting in Ireland. The bag was 162 head. The best day I ever had at Banagher with only four of us shooting. Snipe accounted for the majority of the total, a small number of golden plover and twenty-three duck-billed birds, mostly widgeon and a few pintail. Not only did I shoot my first ever pintail but I managed a right and left of them! It had been a quite remarkable forty-eight hours – I slept most of the way back to Dublin.

Monday morning I had to come down to earth and remind myself that if I didn't get down to some hard work such weekends might not continue. At 3.00 p.m. I set off for Cahir where I was going to spend the night at the hotel before travelling on to Lismore early the next morning. I received a warm welcome from Eileen McCool, had a 'jar' or maybe it was two with Pat John before heading for the dining room. A huge fillet steak was put before me, with chips and fried onions to be followed by an excellent bit of cheese and coffee. I returned to the bar, the only place to sit, full and contented and started to chat with Eileen McCool. She looked around her and then whispered "I have the case of Scotch for you." I thanked her profusely and, at the same time, enquired how the devil I was going to get it through the Irish customs?

We were pondering this knotty problem when I heard a voice behind me. I thought it sounded familiar. "Hallo Eileen and aren't you looking great. Divil a care you can have in the world."

"Father Pat!" Eileen McCool brushed past me. I turned; there stood the hunting priest from Saturday. Miss McCool went to introduce us but my reverend friend was already pumping my arm up and down saying how good it was to see me again. We had a drink. In fact we had several drinks, for it is something they can do well in Ireland and none better than some of the holy fathers! We were busy again riding every ditch of the previous Saturday's hunt when Eileen McCool came and sat down with us.

"I have the answer. Father Pat will take it for you."

"Now hold on. Take what and where?"

"A case of Scotch." The situation was explained.

"No trouble. Don't I owe this man? Didn't he stay with me when me horse was
ditched and in the middle of a great hunt too?"

So it was that late on the afternoon of the 23rd December 1947 I called at one of the leading Catholic Presbyteries in London to collect my contraband. The power of the priesthood in Eire I was to find was great! The ageing father who admitted me was obviously expecting my arrival. I think he thought I'd come to make my confession to Father Pat!

CHAPTER 3

'Strawberry Hill and the Helephant Man'

Christmas came and went. It had been a highly successful three days, although one friend had become very poorly from a surfeit of fillet steak and other Irish goodies! The spirit of Christmas had been reciprocated by the chief agent. When taking delivery of the whisky arrangements had been made for six brace of pheasants to be delivered to the presbytery. Father Pat had confided in me that he had a great weakness for all game birds, to the degree, he assured me, of being sinful.

It seemed that the more work I completed the more there was requiring my attention. However, I enjoyed every minute of it. But to enable me to take full advantage of the wonderful sporting facilities I had to work very long hours. To achieve these I would frequently go into my office which I had now opened in Dublin, not five minutes drive from Dartmouth Road, for two hours before breakfasting at 8.30 a.m. This habit was considered most odd by my friends. To me it was well worth the effort, for I could go off shooting or, indeed, hunting, with a clear conscience.

I quickly learned that in Ireland one did not stand on ceremony. Everyone seemed to know everyone else. As one man I was introduced to in the Shelbourne Rooms put it – "In Ireland you can easily be a big cog in a small wheel; whereas in England if you have a lot of luck, you may become a small cog in a very big wheel." There was, I found, much truth in this. It therefore came as no surprise to me to be approached one day by a complete stranger. It was the beginning of the third week in January and I was on my way back from visiting the Bruree Stud. I had had a hectic day and was several hours later than I had intended getting away. Realising I had no hope of being back in Dublin at a reasonable time for dinner I stopped at a very good steak bar that had recently opened in Limerick. I sat up at the counter and gave my order. It was early and there was only one other customer. He was sitting at the far end. I quietly sipped my drink and cogitated over the day's happenings. There was much to think about.

I suddenly realised I was being spoken to. "Excuse me, but I couldn't help noticing you when you came in. Aren't you the Duke of

Westminster's agent? I saw your photograph in the paper recently."
"Yes."

"I thought as much. We have mutual friends, the Ganlys. I'm Derek Kennedy and I own the Corrib Hotel at Oughterard. It used to be Sweeneys."

I had heard much about Oughterard in Co. Galway, situated on the edge of Lough Corrib. The latter was a vast expanse of water some twenty-three miles long and eleven wide at the maximum point. Further, there were said to be 365 islands in it but I never counted them. It was noted for the brown trout that inhabited its waters in large quantities and in particular for the mayfly fishing. Soon we were deep in conversation. I enquired about the shooting and Derek told me that locally there was nothing that would interest me and could in no way be comparable with the Shannon or Meath. However, if one was prepared to drive for about three quarters of an hour to an hour one could have a reasonable days sport. He went on to tell me that he had recently discovered a wonderful shoot about an hour and a half's drive called Strawberry Hill -very much in the wilds and the home of teal.

It so happened that my brother, Ralph, a tea planter, was home on leave from Assam and was due to join me the following day. I had planned, with the full approval of the chief agent, to take three days off to go shooting with my brother. The more I heard about Derek's hotel and Strawberry Hill the more certain I was that that was where we should go. The hotel I knew was excellent, far removed from the Shannon View.

As we talked I learned that Derek and his wife were leaving for the Bahamas the next day but that he had a most competent manageress who would run things whilst he was away. As far as the shooting was concerned, there were no problems. He said he would put me in touch with Peter O'Farrell who, whilst very much maintaining his independence, looked after the keen fishing and shooting guests who stayed at the hotel. Peter, he told me, was something of a character. His father had been a Colonel in the British Army Medical Corps stationed in India. Like most children, when the time came, Peter was sent home to one of Ireland's top boarding schools. He loathed it and so, quite simply, he ran away.

He made his way across Ireland undetected. Later, when we became close friends, he told me he had travelled by night and slept during the day. For food he had robbed hen roosts and lived off raw eggs, drinking from streams when thirsty. Eventually he arrived on the shores of Lough Mask. He was fishing mad and it was not long before he met up with a near recluse who lived on one of the islands. Peter, after a short while, threw in his lot with his new and highly eccentric acquaintance. The latter was a born naturalist and taught Peter much in this sphere. He also educated his youthful protégé in the finer points of salmon poaching and the art of fly fishing. Peter had an old greenheart rod. In his hands it would become a living entity, for the length of the line he could control and the accuracy with which he could place a fly was quite uncanny.

By the time I'd finished my steak I was hooked. I booked a couple of rooms at Derek's hotel for the Thursday, Friday and Saturday nights. The latter, before he left on his holiday, would arrange for Peter to look after us and shoot Strawberry Hill on the Saturday. I left my new friend with some reluctance to set off on the lonely drive to Dublin, but delighted with the arrangements I had made. Before I departed I made him promise to keep me a room for the mayfly fishing and phone me when the time was right.

The next day I went out to Collinstown Airport and met my brother off the afternoon plane from London. He had taken off from Northolt, the then main London airport for short-haul flights, in a DC-3 that took two and three quarter hours to reach Dublin. He was in good form but gaunt from a recent bout of dysentery. A world separated the carefree days of our youth and those of adult responsibility. We had much to talk about. We dined at the Shelbourne that night and talked and talked.

The next morning, whilst my brother explored Dublin, I frantically worked in the office so as to leave my desk clear before setting off for Galway. It was a road, as yet, strange to me. All I knew was that it was a journey of at least 150 miles, right across Ireland. Nothing in these days of motorways but quite a trek when one had to pass through every town and village with roads not always of the best. We left early in the afternoon. It was not long before the sky blackened, the wind rose and flurries of snow slowed us down to a modest pace. However, about halfway the snow changed to sleet and then to rain. The wind increased and at times I was afraid we would be blown off the road. It was well after seven before we reached our destination and the wind over the last half hour had dropped perceptibly.

I was immediately struck by the warmth and comfort of the hotel. Peter was waiting for us in the bar. Ralph and I, it seemed, were the only residents. After a quick drink we went in for dinner having arranged to meet Peter later. The meal was excellent and the cellar provided a wide choice at most reasonable prices. We returned to the bar where Ralph was delighted to find they had Dewar's White Label whisky – which he assured me was the favourite tipple of tea planters.

As the evening developed several locals, including John Gill, who vied with Peter for being the most successful gillie of the many working out of Oughterard during the trout-fishing season, joined us. Peter was something of an introvert, for his life was organised so as to obtain the maximum of pleasure with the minimum of work; except at what he enjoyed doing, then he gave it his all. Quite simply his life revolved around fishing and shooting. He had never returned to school. It had been three years before he had decided to leave his hideout on Lough Mask and that was only when, by chance, he learned of his father's retirement and return from India. The latter had bought a bungalow a couple of miles outside Oughterard and it was there that Peter was living when I first met him.

Ralph, who was in high spirits, did not allow the assembled company's glasses to remain empty for many seconds. He was, quite obviously, enjoying himself and I quietly congratulated myself on my choice of venues for our few days together. As the evening progressed so the talk turned to bigger targets than snipe and duck. My brother had accounted for a number of killer tigers, leopards and several rogue elephants. Such talk intrigued the few locals, who had the price of a pint and frequented the bar. I remember Peter telling me that the average weekly earnings in the winter for the inhabitants of the village was about seventeen shillings a week. Nearly all relied on the summer tourist trade. The money earned from this had to be carefully eked out over the remainder of the year.

"Tell me sorr an' when did you last shoot a helephant?" The questioner was a wizened little man who had slowly edged himself into the party.

"Oh, about a month ago."

"An' how did you do that?"

No further encouragement was needed. Ralph was a good storyteller. It appeared he'd been having an evening at the Club. Mellowed by Mr. Dewar's most excellent product he had returned to his bungalow. There he found a large number of his labour force assembled and, it was quickly obvious to him, in a great state of agitation. It appeared that about two hours earlier the peace of the lines (village) had been shattered by a ferocious and sudden attack from an elephant. Trumpeting in a most terrifying way it had demolished three mud and bamboo houses and killed four of the inmates. The whole community had fled. The elephant had destroyed several more homes before turning its attention to a nearby rice paddy. That, Ralph was told, was where it still was and would the Sahib please go and shoot it. It was a very dark night and he was not enamoured with the idea of tackling a rogue elephant under such conditions. However, experience had taught him that once a rogue always a rogue!

There was little doubt that this particular one, having had its fill, would return to the lines and reap further devastation. Reluctantly, Ralph went into the bungalow, hastily changed and collected his double-barrelled elephant gun, together with a high-powered torch. Then, having told the assembled crowd to go home and, above all else, keep quiet, he headed for the rice field accompanied by his gun-bearer. The latter had been on many such forays with him, was a hundred per cent reliable and very knowledgeable in all aspects of hunting. As they neared the rice paddy, Ralph did not like what he found. There was no cover; no trees, nowhere to go if things went wrong and the hunter became the hunted!

Stealthily he approached his quarry from down wind, slow step by slow step, hardly daring to breathe. One small mistake could spell disaster, for having already killed four times that evening and goodness knows how many times before, he was under no illusion that the rogue bull would have any compunction about making him number five! As he drew nearer he could hear the swish as the elephant pulled up the rice to feed. At last he judged he was some twenty to twenty five yards away. He could just discern the vast bulk of his target; the thing was which way was it facing. He took a deep breath, dry mouthed, scalp tingling he switched on the torch and within a fraction of a second fired. He had been lucky, for he had been given a perfect opportunity of a brain shot resulting in a clean kill. When he examined the dead elephant he found it had a huge abscess on its anus, some two and a half feet long and half as wide. No wonder the poor creature had become a rogue!

The little old man looked at Ralph for quite a perceptible time before he spoke.

"Be the hokey, I'm thinking I'd be needing to change me trousers if I'd met that fellow." Then giving a mighty grin that disclosed but two blackened front teeth, he turned to the assembled company. "I'm telling you them snipes has no chance." Ralph got him another pint of porter!

Around midnight the door opened and in walked the sergeant and a garda from the barracks on the opposite side of the road. "Good night men. 'Tis getting late and near time you lads went home." No one seemed the least concerned. Closing time was 10.30 p.m. I offered the Sergeant and his companion a drink, both accepted with alacrity and we settled down for another hour or so of chat. Ralph and I had long since ceased to replenish our own glasses – serious shooting and strong drink don't mix.

The next morning we set off just after 9.00 a.m. We would have been ready to go earlier, but Peter, when he'd eventually departed in the early hours, had said there was no rush – hadn't we all the day ahead of us? We motored out to the far side of Galway and, following Peter's instructions, turned down a boreen. As I got out of the car the first thing I saw was a skein of White-fronted geese, coming in to land on a field some three to four hundred yards away which was virtually covered with geese. There must have been at least five hundred. Peter too had seen them.

After assessing the various options and the direction of the wind, he suggested that Ralph and I would position ourselves behind a stone wall that went off at right angles to the boreen. He would make a long detour and come up a ditch hidden by a partially broken down wall behind them and try and drive them over us. With great stealth we took up our position. I noted there was a whitewashed cottage and a few buildings across the small field behind us, a matter of some eighty yards away. It had not been visible when we got out of the car, as it was sheltered by a screen of conifers from the Atlantic gales. It seemed an interminable time before I saw Peter creeping round the patch of gorse beyond the geese. Their cackling and honking made sweet music as the adrenaline flowed. And still they came, skein after skein, one glided over the wall between Ralph and me comfortably in range for him. I prayed fervently that he wouldn't be tempted but, like me, he hugged the wall not daring to look up.

As I watched Peter suddenly appeared beyond our quarry and gave a yell that would have done credit to an Apache brave. With a roar of beating wings and much cackling, a field of geese became airborne. They were heading straight for us! It was then I became aware of someone calling behind us. I glanced round and there, walking straight for the wall where we hid was a man, his collie dog running towards us ahead of him from the cottage. I returned my attention to the geese. They too had seen the intruder and with increasing noise, were climbing fast away to our right. Out of many hundreds of geese not one came within, as they would say in Ireland, an ass's roar of us. The foiler of our plan waved cheerily as he clambered over the wall and called out. "Good day men. Is it shooting you are? There's a heap of geese around so there is. Good luck to you."

With that he was gone across the fields to look at his stock. As I joined Ralph he was saying something in Hindi. I believe it was to do with the lineage of the farmer who had so unwittingly foiled our plan! Peter arrived back, soaked! He had slipped when creeping up the ditch and filled both his waders. However, he remained both cheerful and philosophical over the whole incident, for, as he so rightly said, hadn't a man every right to walk over his own land?

We left the car where it was and continued on down the boreen. Suddenly Peter, who was leading, stopped, signalled us to keep down behind the wall and join him. He whispered that he had spotted a small flock of golden plover going into a field several hundred yards ahead. This led to a backbreaking stalk, for whilst Co. Galway is crisscrossed with dry stonewalls, many are in a bad state of repair and not very high. When we had wriggled and squirmed ourselves into position, at a given signal from Peter, we all stood up. Many hundreds of plover rose into the air. We all managed to get off three shots. The pick-up was seventeen. Peter's Springer collecting the runners, whilst we gathered up the dead birds.

Next our guide took us into an area of some forty acres of briars, hazel and rocks. It was terrible walking, but typical of thousands of acres in the West of Ireland. The spoils were equally divided as we emerged on the far side, somewhat blown, scratched, but each bearing a woodcock; always an exciting addition to the bag whatever the status of the shoot. We made our way back to the car and drove to the main road. Shortly we turned off again down another boreen. When we stopped we were looking down on a wide expanse of marshy fields, with a river running through them. Peter said that, whilst he knew it would be alright to shoot them, he had to go to the house first and ask permission.

Ralph and I accompanied him across a small field to the whitewashed thatched cottage with its few adjoining buildings. A variety of poultry including four turkey hens that had obviously avoided the Christmas festivities were scratching around in the yard. Before we reached the door it opened and the man of the house appeared. He greeted Peter in Gaelic and a conversation followed that we were not privy to. Eventually they reverted to English. Peter told us that it would be alright to shoot the fields.

"Indeed it will, bang away." The owner eyed Ralph and me and then hastily added "But it'll cost a few bob so it will! I produced a pound. "My but aren't you the gentleman? Come in and have a cup, the tae's brewed." Peter looked enquiringly at me. I nodded and in we went. Like so many Irish homes in those days the ceiling and walls were brown from smoke. A turf fire burned brightly, wisps of smoke floating out into the room from the open grate. A huge blackened kettle hung on a hook over the centre of the fire, whilst a pot of tea stewed on the hearth. Children of descending
sizes seemed to be everywhere. Peter introduced us to our host, Sean O'Dwyer and his wife Bridget. The latter wiped her hands on her apron, she was busy making bread, she shook us warmly by the hand and bid us welcome. Sean told us to take a seat and 'not make strange', whilst his wife poured four cups of black steaming tea.

Then she cut thick slices of hot new soda bread and liberally applied butter – it was delicious. The O'Dwyers proved to be easy and amusing company. It was not until Peter enquired as to whether we intended to shoot any more that we made a move.

Sean's marshy fields proved reasonably productive. When we returned to the car we had added eleven more to the bag – 10 snipe and a teal. Ralph was particularly pleased, having shot his first right and left of Irish snipe. He commented on the fact that they were much faster than those he frequently shot in the rice fields in India. It was remarkably warm for nearly the end of January and we sat on the stone wall by the car as we ate the excellent picnic lunch provided by the hotel. Peter regaled us with tales of great catches of brown trout taken from Corrib and of the monsters that inhabited the deep. The latter at least were no fisherman's tale, for there were two mounted and on display in the bar at the hotel. Both were over twenty pounds.

Mentally I promised myself that one day I too would haul forth one of these giants. Apparently they were only ever fished for on flat calm days, when all other forms of fishing were hopeless. The method was to use a well weighted spinner and troll a couple of these behind the boat. Over the years I was to learn just how boring this could be. In fact once I had sampled the monotony of trolling I seldom became involved. Once and once only it paid off. I landed a twelve and a half pounder, but even that did not produce anything like the excitement of a 3 to 4lb fish caught on the wet fly or dap.

After we had finished our lunch, had a smoke and a 'tincture' from the bottle of sloe gin I had put in the car, we drove back towards Oughterard. Peter took us to a number of small marshy holes or, in some cases ditches that had totally silted up. The latter proved the most productive, but none held more than three or four snipe. However, we all shot reasonably well and by the time we were ready to head back for the hotel we had added another fourteen to the bag; giving a total of 45 head. A lovely sporting day, made all the more enjoyable by the variety and the soft splendour of the countryside.

Peter joined us after dinner, chiefly to discuss plans for the morrow. He said we should be away at the latest by 8.30 a.m. for it was a good hour and a half's run to Strawberry Hill. John Gill came in and inevitably the talk turned to fishing. Both he a Peter extolled the excitements of dapping with mayfly but also, they said, if one could stand the cold, fishing a wet fly at the end of March could be most rewarding.

Soon after the mayfly had vanished the salmon started to run and in June, the sandy bay at the mouth of the Oughterard River could be full of salmon waiting for a spate to make their way up the river to spawn. In the late summer great sport could again be had dapping, this time using as bait a grasshopper and daddy longlegs. This Peter assured us was a deadly combination and although one didn't catch as many fish as when dapping with mayfly, those caught, on average, were bigger. Incidentally, in those days, any trout under 2 lbs were returned to the lough. As we talked it seemed that there was limitless scope for those keen on rod and gun! We did not allow the evening to develop into a late night session as had the previous one. Both Ralph and I headed for bed just after 10.30 p.m. our thoughts on the hundreds of teal that Peter promised we would see and indeed shoot, the following day.

We arrived at Strawberry Hill just before 10.00 a.m. It certainly was the back of beyond. We seemed to drive for miles on gravel roads, which, other than the main roads, was the rule rather than the exception in the late forties in the West of Ireland and, indeed, in many other areas. I switched off the engine and wound down the window, there wasn't a sound; not as much as a dog barking or even a pig grunting. I got out. The house and its few outbuildings were virtually an oasis in the middle of a red-bog. The latter is the term used to describe the heather bogs, of which there were vast areas the length and breadth of the country. It is from these that the turf, such a valuable source of fuel is cut. I looked at Peter. "Do you think there is anyone here?"

"Oh yes. I don't suppose old Paddy is up yet. He's not exactly what you would describe as an early riser." He walked over to the door and banged hard on it, shouting something in Gaelic. There was no response. He opened the door and shouted again. This time there was a muffled reply. A further few minutes elapsed before the owner appeared. He was small, partially doubled over. I noticed his hands were knotted with arthritis. He looked as though he had almost withered with age.

He ignored Ralph and me as he held a conversation with Peter in Irish. The latter was not surprising for we were in the heart of the Gaeltacht, where gaelic is spoken within the homes more than English and is the language through which the children were taught at school. However, virtually all are bilingual. It sounded as though Paddy wasn't too happy. Suddenly he shut the door in Peter's face, the latter, laughing, returned to us.

"Paddy's not too pleased at being woken up. He was at a wake until after six this morning. Anyway he received my telegram to say we were coming and he'll be out when he's had a bite to eat. We may as well sit in the car. It's not too hot standing around here." He was right, there was a cold wind coming in off the Atlantic and there appeared to be nothing to break it as far as the eye could see. When we were comfortably settled back in the car I enquired however did one get a telegram delivered to somewhere as remote as Strawberry Hill?

"Oh, a lad brings it out on a motorbike. He's about eleven miles to come from the Post Office. When we found this place Derek Kennedy went and saw the postmaster. He made an arrangement that the boy gets an extra half-crown every time he makes a delivery for us." It was at least another ten minutes before Paddy appeared, clutching a bottle, containing what looked like water. Without a word he offered the bottle to Peter who took a good swig and handed the bottle back.

"That's a drop of good stuff and no mistake." Peter introduced us. Paddy just nodded as Peter went on to tell him that Ralph had probably shot more elephants and tigers than snipe. This was a gross exaggeration, but at least it provoked some interest from Paddy in so far as he eyed Ralph for several minutes without saying a word. Then he offered my unsuspecting brother the bottle. My mind flashed back to my first meeting with Father Pat, but I said not a word. Peter winked at me.

"That's great stuff, take a good swig." Ralph did, his face turned puce, his eyes bulged as he choked, gasping for breath. At last he could speak.

"What the hell is it?"

Peter laughed. "Poteen – mountain dew – about 98% pure alcohol." Paddy stood impassively by. He took the poteen back, had a good gulp, not a muscle even twitched, corked the bottle and put it in his pocket.

Paddy, via Peter, gave instructions not to shoot until we were all in position. We were, he said, heading for what was described as 'A wee hole in the turf, the home of teal.' We made our way out onto the bog, Paddy leading. We had only gone several hundred yards when I could clearly discern the 'wee hole'. It was a pond some sixty to seventy yards long and about half as wide. What made it interesting was that there were quite an abundance of bulrushes and sedge around the perimeter together with some rough grass and gorse. As we drew nearer I could hear the distinctive, almost bell-like call of the drakes. From the noise emanating from 'the hole' it did not sound as though Peter had been exaggerating about numbers.

There were some very rudimentary hides, which I was to learn later Derek, with great difficulty, had persuaded Paddy to build. Peter whispered instructions whilst Paddy headed off to approach the pond from the opposite end to where we were stationed. Heart pounding, I took up my position and made sure the other two were safely installed behind their meagre cover. I had only just checked on this when, suddenly, the air was full of teal. There must have been anything from five hundred to a thousand. They did not fly off after we had fired, but kept circling and coming back to the pond. The others were getting plenty of shooting, but it was patently obvious that I was in 'the hot seat'. I couldn't get the cartridges in quick enough.

Something else was equally obvious – I was shooting abominably. Never had I shot so badly before, nor for that matter, since. The more I missed the worse I became. At last the teal gave up what could have been almost kamikaze attempts to return to their habitat, without any major losses being inflicted by me, and departed out onto the bog. I should and normally would have shot at least thirty to forty teal – I picked five! Paddy was to take the bag back to the cottage, before we started to walk the bog for snipe and, Peter told us, teal. When I handed Paddy my contribution he gave me a withering look and spat with great deliberation.

Some twenty minutes later we were on our way again. My state of mind had not been improved by my dear brother commenting, ad nauseam, on the quality of my shooting, for the majority of the time that Paddy had been absent! We set out across a wide expanse of red-bog, about sixty yards apart. Paddy had placed himself between Peter and Ralph. This too was very pointed. He addressed Ralph and Peter for the first time since we arrived in English. "I'll be with you two men where there'll be some birds to carry."

There was an abundance of snipe sitting tight and normally I would have revelled in the quantity of game. Teal were plentiful too, rocketing into the air from the bog holes, really sporting shots but, alas, my shooting remained abysmal and the more I worried the worse it became. It was getting on for 2.00 p.m. by the time we had done the circuit of the bog and were back at Paddy's dwelling. We were about a hundred yards from this when a very high teal came over; both Ralph and Peter missed with both barrels. As it came over me it was really climbing. I killed it stone dead with my first shot. Some self-respect had been regained. Paddy laid the bag out on the ground – 41 teal and

29 snipe. If I had shot even half of my normal form we'd have had well over 100 head. Peter whispered to me that it was normal practice to give Paddy £1. I gave him three. He took it grimaced and at last spoke to me.

"Thank you sorr, 'tis aisy to see youse not used to shootin'. I'm thinking 'tis the helephants you should be bangin' at." He scratched his head, spat and continued "An I'm thinkin' you'd miss the b......s, even if they lay down for you." Without another word he stalked off into his cottage. Strawberry Hill it might well be, but there had certainly been no cream on my day!

CHAPTER 4

'The Battle of O'Brien's Bridge'

These days the 31st of January would mean the end of the shooting season, but in the forties, snipe and golden plover could be shot, in Ireland, up to the last day in February. Hunting, of course continued well into April. I managed another day with the Ward, but what time I could spare from work in February was mainly utilised for shooting. Days were becoming very limited, for the season would soon be over. It was near the middle of the month when George phoned me. Would I care to shoot at Ballygar on the Galway/Co. Roscommon border on Saturday? I had heard much about the Ballygar shoot from my friends. They had a long lease, on some seven thousand acres, at what could only be described as a nominal rent. There was a rugby football international at Landsdowne Road on the Saturday, which took precedence in 'the house of Ganly' over shooting. George, obviously, wanted a companion. From what I heard Banagher seemed to pale into insignificance by comparison and I was delighted to have the opportunity to visit such a renowned shoot. The answer was, of course, 'yes'.

We left Dublin late in the afternoon on the Friday and drove down to Athlone, staying the night at the Shamrock Lodge Hotel. After an excellent dinner we headed for bed. It was, George told me, just over half an hour's drive to the shoot and he was anxious that we should leave by 8.00 a.m. We arrived at Jim O'Brien, the keeper's cottage, on time. Jim still held the honorary title of keeper, but in fact time, rheumatism and arthritis had caught up with him, making it impossible for him to walk for any great distance. He owned a three roomed cottage and a few small fields adjoining the Sheveen river, a tributary of the Suck, which also ran through the shoot. Behind Jim's cottage was Island Case, a red-bog of some two thousand acres, a noted home of snipe.

This, around the preceding Christmas time, had not escaped the notice of a local priest, new to the locality, who had planned a pleasant afternoon's snipe shooting on the bog over his field trial winning Red Setter. However, he had not considered Jim when making his plans, although he knew of his existence. The latter on hearing shots not far away on Island Case, had gone storming out from his home waving a stick and roaring, so the cleric said, in a most unseemly manner. Jim had threatened prosecution, excommunication, as well as several slow forms of death. Further, he had addressed the priest by his surname. "Father O'Halloran to you."

"Yer black coated b….r," came the quick rejoinder "when you're poaching Mr. McVeagh's bog you're O'Halloran to me."

Jim had grabbed the priest's gun and then literally chased the Holy Father off the bog with amazing agility for an advanced septuagenarian. He abused the priest to such a degree that the poor man sent a formal and harshly worded complaint to George, demanding an apology and his gun back. It was as a solicitor that George replied, threatening the utmost rigour of the law. Further, he enquired how it would look for a priest to be prosecuted not only for poaching, but also for not having a gun licence? The latter was an inspired guess. The priest phoned, full of apologies, could he please have his gun back and promised to get a licence immediately. That was only weeks before I met Jim. For one of such advanced years he certainly was a tough character! How tough I was to learn before I returned to Dublin that night.

I was made most welcome by Jim. He assured me that any friend of Mr. McVeagh's was a friend of his. George and I took the box with our lunch in it, put up by the hotel, into the front room of the cottage, together with our dry clothes. Jim followed us through, extracted a quarter pound packet of tea from the box and returned to the kitchen. Then, to my amazement and horror he opened the packet and emptied the entire contents into a vast kettle already simmering over a turf fire. This, I was to learn, was Jim's way of making a good strong cup of tea! When we were alone I commented to George about it and remarked what a waste. He had replied that it wouldn't be and that Jim would keep the brew going for a number of days!

We were a little handicapped by not having a driver. However, I was to walk the banks of the Sheveen down to what was known as The Iron Bridge, making plenty of sweeps out onto the red-bog. George would meet me at the bridge with the car in about two hour's time. I set off full of great expectations for I had heard so much about Island Case. I had walked a quarter of a mile or more before I even saw a snipe and that jumped at least a hundred yards ahead. There was no wind, what little cloud there had been was now replaced by blue sky and the sun shone brightly. Even with my limited experience I realised it was a hopeless day for snipe shooting. However, there appeared to be an abundance of duck on the river. Further, they remained paddling around in a most tantalising manner until I was well within range. It was as if they knew the season was over!

I began to find a few snipe several hundred yards out on the bog and a number sat long enough to give me some shooting. I faced a big area of the soft springy 'turf' and it was two and a half hours before I reached the bridge. There was no sign of George. I sat down, tipped out my game bag and counted – ten snipe and three golden plover. I was lucky to get the latter. They had been flying the line of the river and cut in over the bog at the bend. I had been out of sight behind a bush, collecting the only snipe that I'd shot on the riverbank.

As I settled down in the warm sunshine a trout rose in the river below, then another. Not big, perhaps three quarters of a pound to a pound, but big enough to arouse my interest, for I had been used to fishing the North Devon rivers where a pound fish was a good one. It was incredibly warm for February. I lit my pipe, took my jacket off and relaxed. It must have been a good half hour before George arrived, but the time went quickly as I watched a number of species of duck fly the line of the river and several skeins of Greylag geese make their way, honking, to the centre of Island Case. All the while there was the background plop-plop of rising trout. The sun had brought on a hatch of fly. I could not make out what they were, but they were being ravenously devoured.

It was with great delight that I discovered I had done better than George. All he had added to the bag in the three hours since we parted were eight snipe. My feeling of superiority was to be short lived for he remarked that he had only seen nine. I had seen at least seven or eight times as many as I had shot and missed at least double that number! We went off and shot several rushy fields and a small section of red-bog. By the time we'd finished we'd only added another seven snipe to the bag. George was most despondent. Twenty-five snipe by lunch was, he claimed, an all time low for Ballygar.

We arrived back at Jim O'Brien's cottage. He had been joined by Jimmy Langan, a smallholder from the other side of the village who acted as part time keeper on that side of the shoot. After we had eaten we took two cups of Jim's brew outside and sat on the garden wall in the sun as we planned the afternoon. Jimmy Langan felt we would find more snipe on the Horseshoe Bog than we had seen in the Island Case area. Old Jim was dubious, claiming that if they weren't on the latter in big quantities, then there were none around. After much debate, in which I took no part, it was decided to take young Jimmy's advice. He came with us. It was getting late when we finished the long trek around the bog – seven miles. Old Jim had been right. Even with George's superb shooting and, I might add, not too bad an effort on my part, we'd only added another seventeen snipe to the tally. Certainly we had not seen more than thirty five to forty the entire afternoon.

As we approached Jim's cottage, we were confronted by the strange sight of 'himself' almost staggering across the road with a huge lump of rock clasped to his chest. Almost falling, he deposited his burden on the parapet of the bridge. It was then that I noticed there were several other great chunks of stone already balanced precariously on the edge. We pulled up and got out of the car. Jim was red in the face, puffing and blowing from his exertions. He looked as though he could pass out at any moment.

George rushed across to him. "Whatever are you doing?"

"Jasus Mr. Mac, am I glad to see you. There's two blaggards away up the river in a boat shooting duck so they are, an' them out of season. I'll sink the b…..s when they come back so I will." He said something to Jimmy Langan in Irish as he added another lump of stone to the ammunition on the parapet. It looked formidable! It would be a fast boat that could get through unscathed when and if they were pushed over the edge. Any one of the rocks would hole and sink a boat immediately. It also occurred to me that should anyone be hit on top of the head with 15 to 20 lbs of granite the prognosis for the recipient's future would not be too rosy!

I voiced my concern to George. However, he did not seem unduly worried and said that he was off to find a member of the Garda Siochana. As he drove off, three shots rang out from up the river; leading to what, I felt sure, was something very explicit in Irish from Jim. Jimmy Langan stood; grim faced, on the bridge, one hand resting on a great lump of rock, ready for action.

The light was going fast and it was obvious that the marauders would soon have to return. George had told me that the boat could only go about half a mile above the bridge. I felt that things could well get out of hand and that, what at this stage was quite an amusing interlude, could well end in tragedy. I decided to walk up to the bend in the river some eighty to a hundred yards above the bridge and call on the intruders, when they returned, to surrender before worse befell them. Jim obviously did not approve of my plan and as I walked away I heard him muttering something about 'bloody sassenachs'.

I took up my position behind a bush, strategically sited on the bend. I had not been there many minutes when I distinctly heard the splash of oars. Jim had said that when the boat went up the river it was powered by an outboard motor. Possibly the poachers thought that a silent approach would get them through the bridge unnoticed. I could see the boat coming down the centre of the river. There were two men in it, one rowing, the other sitting in the stern holding a gun. When they were nearly opposite I stepped out from behind the bush and shouted for them to pull in to the bank. With an oath, the one on the oars quickened his stroke whilst his companion pointed his gun in my direction. I ran down the bank, shouting at them to stop, but they paid no heed.

The boat must have been about three lengths from the bridge, when up popped Jim and young Jimmy and started pushing rocks off the parapet. I heard old Jim shouting "Sink the b…..s, drown t'em." For a moment I thought the two men were going to try and make a run for it. Fortunately their nerve failed them. Turning, they managed to run their boat ashore on the far bank, just out of reach of Jim's missiles.

At the same moment as the two poachers stepped onto dry land, George drew up and two gardai got out of the car. The battle of O'Brien's bridge was over! Guns, ammunition and eleven duck billed birds were taken off the offenders, amid much cursing and swearing. When the hubbub had died down we learned that there was a third member of the party on an island about three quarters of a mile down stream. Jim was all for leaving him there and he had to be forcibly stopped from holing the boat with a rock to ensure this happened. Eventually young Jimmy and a garda went off in the boat and collected the third miscreant. He had four more duck. It was quite a while before all the formalities were completed and the 'prisoners' allowed to depart.

Their guns and cartridges together with the ducks were impounded by the gardai. George wanted to keep the boat, but this eventually was decided against, although it would have been quite legal. The general feeling was that, once everyone had gone, Jim would break it up for firewood! That, the gardai said, would not help our cause when the case came to court. As it turned out, it might have been the best thing. The judge, whilst finding the offenders guilty on a number of charges was lenient to an extreme and, in total, fined them ten shillings each! Such was my introduction to Ballygar. In the years to come, when I became a member of the syndicate, never did we shoot less, but equally, never did we have such a dramatic end to a day!

The weeks rushed by. I only managed one more day's snipe shooting before the close of the season; although I did manage the odd hour in what I now considered as 'my marshes', around Maynooth. Working for the Duke was, in every respect, great. However, I was discovering that one's personal life was not allowed to interfere with his wishes. Sunday to him was as good a working day as Monday.

A major event in the Irish Farming Calendar was the Spring Show organised by the Royal Dublin Society at Ballsbridge. This is always held during the first week in May. A number of the Duke's Shorthorns were being exhibited for the first time in Ireland and it was an absolute MUST that I was there for the majority of the week. It had been a warm dry spring, everything was very forward. Imagine then my disappointment when, on the Monday evening of show week, I received a phone call from Derek Kennedy. "The Mayfly are up and plentiful". He had a room reserved for Peter and me, plus of course his boat, booked for me from Wednesday until the weekend. My disappointment at not being able to go was intense, but I was slightly mollified by the fact that one of the exhibits from Maynooth won the Supreme Championship at the show. The first time this had ever been achieved by a Dairy Shorthorn. Champagne flowed, as did congratulatory telegrams from the Duke. So pleased was he, that I was an invited to cross over on the Holyhead ferry to be his guest at Chester races, which always, I was to find, clashed with the Spring Show and return on the ferry that night.

I had found I never really slept on the ferry and, if I couldn't go fishing, I was damned if I was going to go without two nights sleep just to go racing! The trouble was one didn't say no to the Duke. My secretary and I spent a considerable time composing a suitable reply. It was all to do with how much I would like to accept BUT it was terribly important for the future of the herd that I should be at the show. Success! I received a three page reply which, basically, was commending my devotion to duty!

As the estates developed, so my workload increased and I spent much time in England attending meetings and various other functions. I gave up using the ferries and started to fly Aer Lingus. As with everything else in Ireland, everyone knew everyone. Quickly I became a 'regular' on the DC3s that plied between Eire and Great Britain. On several occasions, when I was suddenly summoned to cross the Irish Sea and was pressed for time, the Company would obligingly hold the plane until I arrived at Collinstown. Such was the charm of Ireland in the forties. It was an exhilarating and challenging life; it was also, at times, exhausting.

Towards the end of June I felt I must have a short break and arranged a long weekend at Oughterard. I arrived there on a Thursday evening to a warm welcome from both Derek and Peter. Fishing prospects were not good. They never were for a few weeks after the 'dap' had ended. However, Peter was confident that I should get a few trout on the wet fly, providing there was a wind. Friday dawned bright and still and remained so the entire day, the sun beating down relentlessly as I made my debut trolling. I was not impressed. From a fishing point of view it was a dead loss, but as a mode of relaxation it had much to commend it. I made myself comfortable in the bottom of the boat, a rod out either side and, well cushioned with rolled up oilskin coats, slept. At lunch time we landed on one of the many islands, built a fire, boiled a kettle and made tea; having had something stronger to start with, and lay in the sun and chatted. The heat was such that we might easily have been in the South of France.

On Peter's insistence we again went forth onto the flat calm lough – there wasn't a ripple! I again took up my position in the bottom of the boat, the gentle movement of it's progress quickly lulled me back to sleep. I dozed for most of the afternoon. Suddenly I was wide awake, being exhorted by Peter to strike. I picked up the rod and did as I was bid. The rod bent nearly double and line screamed off the reel as Peter frantically reeled in the other line. This was better. There was no doubt that I was into a weighty fish. Peter beamed. "I told you it was worth trying." After a couple of wild dashes the fight seemed to go out of my captive and it became a question of 'pumping' it up from the depths. I looked at Peter.

"I don't think this is a monster trout. It certainly doesn't fight like one."

The smile had left Peter's face. "Afraid you're right. My bet is it's a pike. If only we could exterminate them, the trout fishing would be even better than it is." Two or three minutes later he was proved right as he netted a 17½lb pike which he quickly dispatched. Out went the lines again. I filled my pipe and sat quietly in the stern deep in thought as Peter continued to paddle slowly round. My daydreaming was interrupted as a salmon leaped high in the air, landing with a splash. That was more like it. A big grin spread across Peter's face.

"They've started to run. I saw them in the river, waiting to come up the lough last week when I was in Galway." I enquired what the chances of catching one were. Peter told me that the best hope was the sandy bay at the mouth of the Oughterard river, but one must have a good wave. It was hopeless without wind, for it was very shallow. As he said this a ripple appeared on the vast expanse of water all around us. I looked towards the west, a few streaks of cloud stretched across the azure blue sky. I felt a puff of wind on my cheeks. I started reeling in one of the lines.

"What are you doing?"

"Peter, I've had enough of this, let's head for home. If, and I know it's a big if, there is any wind when we reach the bay, let's do a couple of drifts." The light puffs of wind were beginning to turn into a gentle breeze. I wound in the second line, Peter started up the outboard engine and we headed for the bay. By the time we reached it the water was quite choppy. I had put my fly rod up en route and, with Peter's help, selected a couple of flies. He advised using a 'dropper' as well as a 'tail' fly.

Unfortunately Peter had not got his rod with him. I suggested we should go in and get it. He looked at the sky and shook his head. Better, he said, make the most of the wind, it wouldn't last. We started our drift. I shot out a good length of line and slowly worked it back. I wondered, should I be lucky enough to hook a salmon, how long it would take to land it, for the rod I was using was not meant for salmon. My fourth or fifth cast was to give me the answer. I had the line half in, the dropper bouncing on the wave when 'bang' a lovely head and tail rise and I was into my first Corrib salmon.

The rod bent double, the line screamed out. I was glad I had added plenty of backing to the silk fly line. Peter started to row the boat after the fish as the line cut through the water. Suddenly the salmon jumped. Peter shouted, "Drop the point of your rod." But I was ahead of him. Four more times a silver flash appeared in the air, but at last it was tiring. Slowly I gained line. Peter reached for his big landing net but, as it entered the water, the salmon made one more run. Five minutes later it lay in the bottom of the boat – 7 lbs exactly. A fresh run fish with sea lice still on it.

Flushed with success I reached into the lunch basket and pulled out the half bottle of scotch I had included – just in case! As I passed the bottle to Peter, I realised that the wind had gone, there wasn't a ripple! Luck had certainly been with us. It was only a short distance to the river and the moorings. My companion very quietly paddled the boat in towards the shore. We saw a number of salmon lying on the sandy bottom. Peter advised not to tell anyone about the salmon for, he said, if it was known the salmon had arrived and there was any wind on the morrow, the bay would be full of boats.

That evening, after dinner, feeling much rested and secretly elated, I longed to boast of my success as an enjoyable evening was spent in the bar. There were several other guests on a fishing holiday from England and a number of gillies came in around nine o'clock, including John Gill. Derek's till rang merrily as great fish were caught and lost once again. Peter and I retired early. We had arranged to meet at 5.30 am to fish the bay. Alas, for the want of a little wind the best laid plans of fisherman can go awry! There wasn't a breath. Peter rowed the boat into the bay, but we never bothered to put up the rods. There wasn't even the suspicion of a ripple on the surface. To make it more infuriating we saw a number of salmon jump. Sadly, I returned to the hotel for breakfast, having arranged to meet Peter again at the boat soon after 9.00 a.m.

We sat hopefully waiting. There wasn't a trace of wind. Peter tried hard to persuade me to go off trolling and kept reiterating, "You never know your luck." I had a fair idea. After about an hour Peter, realising he wasn't going to win, suggested that we get in the car and go and try a small lough, away back in the mountains beyond Maam's Cross, which he assured me was teaming with small brown trout. He had never fished it, but knew the man who owned it and for ten shillings it was ours for the day, plus a boat. Fifteen minutes later we were heading out of Oughterard on the Clifden road towards the rugged grandeur of Connemara. Some half hour and twenty miles later, Peter asked me to pull-up opposite and small whitewashed thatched cottage.

As we got out of the car, a man appeared from the only outhouse. He greeted us in Irish and then, as a mark of courtesy towards me, lapsed into English. After a chat I handed over a ten shilling note plus another for good measure, and we were on our way. Some three miles beyond the cottage I drove the car off the road onto a crude parking space that had been cut out of the turf bank. I took the fishing tackle I required out of the back, our lunch and the all important Guinness for my companion. The latter said we had about a two mile walk across the bog on a path marked by hazel sticks set fifty to a hundred yards apart. It was a gorgeous morning, the sun beating down, even more than it had the day before.

In whichever direction one looked there was nothing to be seen but red-bog and mountains, with the Twelve Pins and the Maumturks towering in the distance. Connemara has a harsh but awe inspiring beauty that I grew to love, whatever its mood. As we trudged across the soggy turf Peter told me, quite unnecessarily, that whatever I did not to step into one of the innumerable watery bog holes. I had already been well and truly warned by my snipe shooting friends. Every red-bog is dotted with them, like an uneven colander. Normally, walk into one of these and there is no return, particularly if you are on your own!

Peter told me how, only a couple of years before, two English ladies had gone out to the very lough for which we were heading to paint. They had said they were particularly anxious to capture the magnificence of the sun setting behind the distant mountains. Liam Joyce, the owner of the lough, had warned them to leave in plenty of time so they could make the return journey in daylight. They had parked their car where I had left mine and were seen heading for the lough. That was the last that was ever seen of them. There can be little doubt that, being so engrossed in their painting, they lost all sense of time and left it too late to start out on their return journey. They totally vanished.

We arrived at our destination. The lough looked deep, black and was fringed with granite boulders, in fact, typical of hundreds that exist throughout the West of Ireland. We found the boat, half full of water. A quick examination confirmed what Peter had anticipated. It was barely 'seaworthy'. However, there was a large tin for bailing and whilst I put up my rod, Peter put many gallons of water back where it belonged. As he did this, he told me that a three quarter pound trout would be a monster for these waters. It was therefore decided that nothing would be kept under eight inches in length. I had a measuring tape in my fishing bag and cut a stick of the required length from a nearby scrub bush. At last we were off.

I had put three flies on my cast. As the line snaked out for the first time I could not help thinking that conditions could not have been worse – bright sun and a flat calm. As the flies landed on the water there was a swirl and the rod bent. I was into a fish, but it seemed as though it must be more than three quarters of a pound the way it fought. However, in a very short time I had the answer. I had hooked three! Sport was fast and furious. Peter was kept busy unhooking, measuring, putting fish back and most important, bailing! After a couple of hours I suggested lunch. We went ashore, not that we had left the latter by many yards, neither of us had much faith in our craft!

As we ate, soaking up the hot sun, I marvelled at the incredible quiet. It was almost eerie. Just as I was thinking this I heard the 'cronk cronk' of a raven. I looked up and five were passing overhead, many thousands of feet up, riding the thermals. After about an hour and a half Peter suggested I should have another go. I offered him the rod, but he wouldn't hear of it. I set to again, the ferocity of these little mountain trout seemed unabated. I said I thought we'd caught enough, but Peter urged me to continue saying that if I did not want them, my catch would be very welcomed by some of the older people of Oughterard. So, rather grudgingly, I continued to cast.

Then suddenly, like turning off a tap, it was all over. I kept on for a good half hour and never moved a fish. We took the boat back to where it was kept and, whilst I took down my rod, Peter counted the catch. Forty-seven trout of eight inches or over which, when subsequently weighed, turned the scales at 29½ lbs. He told me that I had in fact caught one hundred and seven trout of varying sizes – some could not have been more than three or four inches. We called at Liam Joyce's, he offered us tea, which was gratefully accepted. It was far removed from old Jim's 'blocky stuff', Liam told us he did not drink alcohol, not even poteen, but did indulge himself when it came to tea. Apparently he took the bus into Galway once a month. There was a service to and from Clifden every day, except Sundays. Each time he always bought several pounds of the very best tea available. Years later I met a man who was in the wholesale tea business. He told me that the greatest connoisseurs and the most discriminating clients he had were in the West of Ireland. Quality, he said, was essential in that part of the country and most definitely appreciated.

Sunday, alas, proved to be yet another gorgeous day. Peter called in at the hotel after he had been to mass. Tentatively he suggested we should go off trolling or what about another visit to Liam Joyce's lough! I declined both and instead made one of my own. What about a drive into Galway? I had never seen the town itself and understood it had much of historical interest to offer. After one more half hearted attempt to get me out onto Corrib, Peter happily acceded.

We strolled around the hot streets until around midday when the open door into a nice cool bar drew us like a magnet. Peter had his usual pint of porter whilst I had a pint of shandy – it was actually cold! Having slaked our thirst we headed for the bridge over the river running out of Corrib. We sauntered out to the middle. The granite parapet is worn smooth by people, who, for centuries, have leaned over to look at the salmon. The river, except when in spate, is only a few feet deep and gin clear. We peered over, the water seemed alive with salmon. Most of them I guessed were six or seven pounders, companions to the one I had caught on Friday, but here and there could be seen slightly bigger ones scattered amongst their fellows. Several locals gazed into the water as they too lazed in the sun. There are few things more peaceful than a river and although in the heart of the town this was no exception. I succumbed to the tranquillity of my surroundings and dreamed of catching all the salmon I could see! Suddenly my reverie was broken by a nudge from Peter.

"Look!" he pointed straight down below were we stood. A real whopper had appeared; it must have been at least fifteen or sixteen pounds. As I watched I became aware of movement to my right. A wizened little man was making his way slowly across the bridge, peering intently into the river. He was an odd sight for his suit was many sizes too big for him. The trousers protruded over worn rubber books, like plus-fours, and the cuffs of his jacket were turned back at least four inches. He wore an old tweed hat pulled well down over his ears. He edged closer, until he was nearly touching me. The smoke from the butty little clay pipe he held clenched between his teeth drifted up into my face – it was strong stuff! Then I heard him draw in his breath, his gaze riveted on the big salmon below us. He looked up.

"Would yer honour stand aside a wee bit?"

"Certainly, but why?"

He took the pipe out of his mouth, knocked out the dottle and carefully put the pipe in the breast pocket of his jacket. "Well sorr, 'tis like this. I'm going to take the big fella there below so I am, an I has to be right above him."

I felt Peter give my arm a tug as he whispered. "Now you'll see something you've never seen before." We moved a few yards further along the bridge and watched. The little man looked intently at the big salmon for several minutes. Then, having taken a furtive look left and right, he undid his coat. He produced a length of cord, it looked like part of a hand-line for sea fishing; attached to the end was the largest treble hook I had ever seen. The actual hooks were painted white. Wrapped around the line, some four inches above the hook was a substantial lead weight. One more look in both directions and the missile went hurtling down. As quickly as it went so it was being hauled back, but on the end was the big salmon, foul hooked some eight or nine inches from the tail. Over the parapet it came and literally disappeared flapping, line and all, down inside the miscreants trousers. He clasped his coat around him and turned to us.

"I'm obliged gentlemen. Isn't he the great one? May God be with you." With that he was off at a shambling run, the salmon still visibly flapping down inside the trouser leg!

One of the locals spat into the river and turned to me. "'Tis terrible sad about Pat John, 'tis an illness he has so it is, taking the salmons. He's only home two days after the last one."

"Home from where?"

The local looked at me as though I was soft in the head. "From prison, where else? Doesn't everyone know that his honour Judge Donovan shut Pat John away for two months for taking an ol' salmon or two. I'm telling you this fishing is a terrible disease so it is!"

CHAPTER 5

'Black Chocolate and Snipe'

The weeks flew by at a quite alarming rate, as did the Irish countryside, as I raced from one ducal property to the next! The vision I had had prior to moving to Ireland of peaceful weekends quietly fishing a well stocked river or lough remained, largely, a figment of my imagination! I just hadn't the time. I envied John Lynch, the gillie at Lismore; part of his job was to fish the Duke's stretch of the famous Blackwater river. The salmon John caught were sent as gifts to the Duke's friends in Ireland. The irony was that John was being paid for doing something I would dearly have loved to have done for nothing!

It was the beginning of September that I arrived down at Cahir to spend the night at the hotel. I received the usual friendly welcome from Eileen McCool and, later, from her brother Pat John. The latter said he was surprised I had planned my visit for that particular night. I enquired why? It appeared that next day was the monthly Fair when a large number of cattle, pigs and a few horses would be congregated in The Square from an early hour. My room overlooked the latter and sleep after 4.00 a.m. would be impossible! Well I was there; certainly I wasn't going back to Dublin so I would have to put up with it.

Apart from the pedigree Shorthorns, a large number of commercial store and beef cattle came under my jurisdiction. I bought and sold around a thousand head in the course of a year. I wanted forty good store bullocks for the stud farm in England. I might well obtain some of these in the morning, if any good cattle were on offer. There was one snag, I hadn't made any arrangements with the local bank to cash a cheque. Most transactions were strictly cash. I mentioned this to Pat John. He assured me there would be no problem, and left the bar. He was back in less than five minutes accompanied by a man who I was to learn was his bank manager. The latter assured me that there would be no trouble about cashing a cheque for as much as I needed and that he would be delighted to have His Grace as a client.

He insisted on cementing good relations in the bar, for the next hour or so! He had a formidable swallow. I couldn't keep up with him. In fact I didn't try! It was well after eleven before I headed for bed. Admittedly early by Irish standards, but I knew I was in for a short night. This, however, might be all to the good. I had put the gun in the car, plus a pair of waders. It had been my intention, if I got through in good time at Lismore, to shoot a number of little marshes close to the main road on my way home. I had been doing some research during the summer and had permission in all cases to 'bang away'. So the earlier I started, the earlier I'd finish and the more time I'd have to shoot.

It was about half three when the noise in The Square became so great that, reluctantly, I accepted the fact that there was nothing to be gained from remaining in bed. Before leaving the hotel I donned my waders. A large concentration of cattle are apt to be somewhat messy and, not infrequently, if they have been grazing good strong lattermarth grass, their range can be phenomenal! It was as well to be prepared!

The centre of The Square was already nearly full with horse and pony carts loaded with pigs. They seemed to range from bonhams (weaners) through porkers, baconers, to old sows. The latter were, no doubt, destined to become sausages or even pork pies. There was much talk, waving of arms, spitting on and smacking of hands as deals were struck. Things were definitely hotting up in the pig section. Many of the shops around the perimeter of the square had their windows boarded up. A wise precaution for the cattle were all herded against the surrounding buildings, kept there by their owners, aided by an army of small boys, all brandishing sticks. I strolled quietly round, hoping I might find what I was looking for.

I saw nothing that took my fancy until I had gone more than halfway round and there, held up in a corner were fifteen lovely quality white head bullocks (Hereford cross). They'd cost about £46 a head in the Dublin sales but would lose at least two stone on the journey, so their country value was around £40 to £42.

The owner saw me looking at them and sidled up. "Good day sorr. Them's great beasts so they are." I nodded and walked round them. He was right, they were like peas in a pod, a rich deep colour, full of quality. The owner followed me. "I'm telling you there's none better in Co. Tipperary an' to yer honour I'd take fifty pounds so I would."

I looked him straight in the eye. "I'm sure you would. I'll give you £36". I had quickly learned in Ireland that if only for the peace of mind of the vendor, one must never give the amount asked, even if the price was right, which it wasn't in this case. If one did, the latter would worry for weeks that he might have got a few shillings more!

"Is it ruined you'd have me? One price sorr and one only - £46." I shook my head and started to walk away.

Buying cattle in an Irish fair was all a matter of bargaining and bluff. As I turned I came face to face with a well known cattle dealer who frequently bought bullocks for the Bruree Stud. He greeted me warmly and asked if I'd join him for 'a quick one'. All the pubs were open and doing a brisk trade. Much to his disappointment I declined. He then set to work trying to make a deal between me, and the owner of the cattle, whose name, I discovered, was Sean Rafferty. After half an hour I made a final offer - £42, providing he gave a good 'luck penny', always an essential of any deal in Ireland. I knew it was probably ten shillings to a pound too much but I would give more in Dublin and they were top quality. Still Sean stuck out for more. I lost interest and after another quick look around the Fair to make sure I wasn't missing anything I collected my things from the hotel, my car from Pat John's garage and headed for Lismore.

It was a gorgeous morning as I drove across to Clogheen wondering if I could get in some shooting before I breakfasted at 'the big house'. There wasn't a soul to be seen as I made my way through the village and headed up over the Knockmealdowns. Just before I reached The Gap a pack of eight grouse rose from the side of the road where, I presumed, they had been dusting. It was a pleasing and most unusual sight. It was just half six as I crossed the bridge over the Blackwater. I had a good two to two and a half hours to shoot.

On impulse, I decided to drive round by John's cottage. The chances of his being up were very remote, but it would only take a few minutes. To my surprise there he was, standing at the door, mug of tea in hand, enjoying the early sun. His astonishment at seeing me at that hour was only equalled by his obvious pleasure.

"Good day sorr. I was just thinking about you. There's a great run of grilse, so there is. Have you a rod with you?"

"No, I'm afraid not."

"Divil a worry, haven't I all a man could want belonging to His Grace. Will you be having a cast or two before breakfast?"

I replied that I thought that was an excellent idea. Five minutes later we were driving out of Lismore on the Fermoy road. After about two miles I drew up at a gateway. Whilst I pulled on my waders, John put up a rod. I donned an old shooting coat I had in the car and we set off across the marshy fields to the river. On the way a number of snipe jumped, all well within range. The river was still coloured after a recent spate and I doubted if I would have any joy.

John, however, was full of optimism and said he was confident I would be lucky as I started to fish the pool down. He was right. About the tenth cast I was firmly into a grilse. It went mad, tearing off up stream into the fast flowing shallows at the head of the pool jumping like something possessed! Quickly I got control and brought it back into deeper water. Within a few minutes of doing that it was played out. I turned to John. He had forgotten the landing net! He told me not to worry and to bring the fish on down to where there was a sandy beach. I did this and he waded into the river, coming round behind the grilse. Suddenly he plunged both arms into the water and with a movement, half scoop half flick, sent the fish flying onto the grassy bank. My first Blackwater salmon and it was a lovely fresh run one, still with sea lice on it and turning the scales at exactly five pounds.

After a quick smoke I started to fish again. This time all that was needed was one cast. Several minutes later a duplicate of the first one lay beside it on the bank. I looked at my watch. I still had an hour before I need think about breakfast.

"Right John, we'll call that a day as far as fishing is concerned. I'm going to walk the rushy fields for snipe".

John grinned. "Aren't you a divil for the sport?"

We went back to the car and I swapped rod for gun. Because time was limited I told John, who was a competent driver, to bring my car to the far end of the fields. Fortunately what little wind there was would be in my back. There was a good sprinkling of snipe, all home bred, sitting very tight and offering easy shots. I was less than a hundred yards from the car when, out of a ditch, five teal rocketed into the sky. I claimed two, but alas not a right and left. I missed hopelessly with the first barrel but bagged two with the second. When I emptied my pocket I had eleven snipe. These, a brace of teal and two grilse by 8.40 am couldn't be bad! It was in fact a feat I was never able to repeat.

I shot more snipe in the years to come by that hour of the day and indeed teal, but was never able to catch grilse as well. I dropped John off at his cottage, had breakfast, met the farm manager and got down to business. Everything was going to plan. At last things were beginning to fall into place and the pressure of the last ten months was easing off. We were through in good time and I was in high spirits as I set off on the 148 mile drive home, thinking of all the marshes I would have time to shoot. The only thing that niggled slightly was that I hadn't been able to do a deal with Sean Rafferty, for they were lovely quality bullocks, just what I was looking for.

As I drove into The Square on my way through Cahir it was almost deserted except for the men with fire hoses washing down the street. As I rounded the corner there was Sean still with his fifteen bullocks. I pulled up and leaned out of the window.

"Not sold them then?"

"Am I pleased to see you. Haven't I been holding these beasts all these hours, not wanting anyone but yer honour to have them. They're yours for £42 so they are." "Hold on, that was this morning. I don't want them now. There are no lorries and the banks are closed. I'm not interested."

Sean gave a tired smile. He looked worried and exhausted. "Aren't I the soft one not knowing who you was this morning? A cheque'll do nicely an' isn't Micky Lyons still here, his lorry is empty, so it is, an' him waiting in Mulligans." I knew Micky Lyons. He often did work for me. He lived only a few miles from the Maynooth estate. If he was going back empty, he'd do the run for a real cut price. To hell with it, I'd wasted enough time over Rafferty's cattle, my mind was on snipe.

"I'll give you my first offer - £36 and that's it."

I started to put the car into gear, then stopped. I couldn't believe what I was hearing.

"'Tis robbery so it is, but, be the hokey, I'll give them to you." Just then Micky Lyons appeared and walked across the square. I got out of the car.

Micky shook me warmly by the hand and then steered me away from Sean and whispered. "He's a terrible decent little man an' that's the truth. Scratches a livin' out of a little ole place that's near all bog. An' there's snipe there as big as turkeys so there are!" Micky winked, he was a likeable rogue and knew my weakness. Then as an after thought, "He's married to my sister so he is."

I moved back to Sean. "Alright, I'll take them, but I can only give you a cheque." "That's alright, isn't it safer than the cash, for I'll not be tempted to have a jar wit' the likes of Micky here." I wrote out a cheque at £4 a head more than Sean had accepted. It didn't feel right working for the richest man in Great Britain to rob a small working farmer. £40 was a fair price on both sides. Sean was delighted and insisted on giving me ten shillings a head 'luck penny'.

I bought Sean's cattle at his farm for many years after that, always in the early part of September. He would never put a figure on them. Having looked at them carefully I would go off and think about the price. It usually took me about three hours to come up with the answer, which, by some strange coincidence, was just about the time it took to shoot the excellent snipe marshes around Sean's home!

Early the following week, George asked me if I would like to shoot at Banagher at the weekend. He and Jim planned to go down on the Friday evening and shoot Saturday and Sunday. Alas, Sunday was out as far as I was concerned, for I had already arranged to fly to London, but Saturday was fine. Obviously I would have to go under my own steam, but, as it happened, that would work in very well. I was due at the stud at Bruree on the Friday and it was no great distance from Limerick to Banagher. I arrived at the Shannon View soon after six, at least an hour before Jim and George could be expected. I put my things in my room and strolled through to the bar. Danny had just walked in. I bought him a drink and settled down to hear the latest prognosis on the shooting front.

Danny was a great talker, particularly after a couple of pints of porter! I can't remember how the conversation turned to hotels. Had Mr Jimmy ever told me about the time that he and the rest of the party had decided to stay at Dooley's Hotel in Birr instead of Banagher? I replied that the occasion had never been mentioned. It appeared that at the time great publicity had been given to the fact that Dooley's was being enlarged and completely renovated. Danny took a mighty swig at his porter, wiped the back of his hand across his mouth and grinned. I knew I was in for a story. Apparently on the previous visit to the Shannon View, George had complained that his bed was damp and in a moment of pique had insisted they should stay somewhere else in the future. So for their next visit to the Shannon, they had booked in at Dooley's.

The party consisted of George, Jim and his brother Willie. The foyer of the hotel was very smart with a nice new reception desk, there was even a hall porter named Mick. George, for some reason, stopped chatting with the receptionist whilst the others went upstairs. Mick, who I was later to come to know well, opened the doors to three of the new rooms with a flourish and told them to take their pick. Two of the rooms were fully decorated, the walls of the third were untouched and great streams of wet ran down the fresh plaster. All the rooms had 'electric bells for service' as Mick proudly pointed out as he dumped George's gear in the uninviting third room. When the latter eventually arrived, he eyed the room but said not a word. Willie told him he should be happy now, he could even ring for room service! It so happened that my friends were planning an early morning duck flight and had come complete with waders and oilskin coats, items of clothing normally spurned. Danny looked pointedly at his empty glass. I ordered a refill.

"Well doesn't Mr. Mac put on his waders, oilskin coat, even his sou'wester, so he did an' then climbs onto the bed. He lays there ringin' the bell."

In no time at all Mick is there. "An' what can I do for you sorr? Isn't them bells great yokes so they are an' isn't yer honour the first to use one." Danny took another swig at his porter before continuing.

"Who," says Mr Mac, waving towards the wall, "who do you think is going to sleep here?"

Mick had apparently scratched his head and pondered the question for a while before with, what Willie had described later, (both he and Jim were in the room) as a satisfied smile he replied "Whichever of you's the strongest!" With that he was gone. After a very brief discussion the three had left for the known and accepted discomfort of the Shannon View. Dooley's had been, like some Spanish hotels today, a little premature with their bookings. In later years I often stayed there. It was and as far as I know still is, a warm and comfortable hotel.

Just as Danny finished his narration, Jim and George walked in. The latter was somewhat disgruntled and most concerned. We were into the second week in September and he hadn't shot a snipe! Normally he and Jim always went out on 1st September but, for the first time ever, the pressure of work had made this impossible. It seemed that he was not at all sure that work should be allowed to interfere with pleasure. He brightened perceptibly when Danny remarked. "An' hasn't it been a great summer for the snipes. They're so thick on the ground you could walk on t'em." Just as we had received this cheering news Rose came through to say the food was on the table, so it was. The menu had not changed!

Having completed our meal we decided to walk out to the bridge a hundred yards or so. It was a lovely warm evening as we leaned against the parapet gazing down into the water. Jim said he wanted some shaving cream. We strolled in a leisurely fashion up the street to the chemist's. It was no surprise to find it open although it was nearly nine o'clock. In those days in Ireland, particularly in the more remote country areas, shops stayed open virtually whilst there was business to be done on a Friday and Saturday night. Jim and I stood chatting to the owner as George browsed around the shop.

Suddenly we heard him exclaim. "Ah, black chocolate. I love that." He picked up a large slab and moved across to pay for it. As he put it on the counter I saw what it was – Exlax! I opened my mouth to speak, but got a quick kick on the ankle from Jim.

"What do you want that for?" he enquired.

"Oh, I often get peckish during the morning. This should keep me going."

Jim grinned. "Yes, that's very possible."

We said good night to the chemist and made our way back to the hotel. Bill had arrived and, making sure that neither he nor Danny would be short of a drink for the evening, we had one quick one and headed for the discomfort of our beds. We wanted to make an early start for being the beginning of the season, there would be several courtesy calls to make, to get confirmation to 'bang away' before we shot some of the places we planned.

We had finished breakfast by eight o'clock. It was a lovely morning, blue sky and a strong south westerly wind, that all important factor when shooting snipe. Bill was waiting by the car when we went out. Jim and George gave their dogs a run and, having collected Danny, it was decided to shoot Clarke's first. This entailed calling at the house and, after a few pleasantries with the owner, we were on our way. George and I took the larger section whilst Jim went off on his own on the opposite side of the boreen. There was a good showing of snipe, but they were surprisingly wild. However, in spite of this, when we met about half an hour later we had eighteen snipe, two teal – a right and left that Jim had had to start the season and, much to Danny's delight, an 'ole green neck' that I had managed to add to the bag.

I often thought that Danny secretly considered mallard and widgeon the only things we shot that were really worth bothering about! After the usual wrangling between Jim and George as to where we should go next it was decided to shoot the callows adjoining the river Brosna; a vast area of flat, poor quality grassland dotted with a few gorse bushes and crisscrossed with drains. Further discussion then took place regarding which way it should be walked, for the wind would be blowing across the callows from the river. Whilst this was taking place George produced his packet of 'black chocolate' and broke off a couple of squares. "Lovely, any one like some?" We all declined.

"You don't know what's good for you. Nothing like a bit of black chocolate to keep you going and give a man energy." He broke off two more squares and popped them into his mouth. "Well, come on, we'll not shoot snipe standing around here." With that he got into the car helping himself to yet another square before putting the packet back in his pocket.

Bill shook his head and turned to Danny. "Be the hokey now, Mr. Mac must have a terrible blockage."

"I'm thinking it won't be for long. I'm telling you, he'll no be short of energy in certain quarters." Grinning broadly Danny climbed into the car and we were off. Having reached the end of the boreen leading onto the callows, Danny got out and opened the old iron gate. We made sure that Bill had safely turned and was back on the hard before setting off. George said he would shoot the section nearest to the river, which was a good half to three quarters of a mile away. I was to take the middle and Jim the top where there was some farmland, but also a number of patches of gorse, all concealing marshy little holes, much favoured by snipe. Danny said he would accompany me although he normally went with Jim. As we took our positions Danny remarked to me that we would have a great view of all that would be going on. The significance of this comment was not immediately apparent to me; my mind was wholly on snipe. We'd been going for about twenty minutes and getting loads of shooting when Danny suddenly broke my concentration.

"Isn't that the quarest thing Mr. Mac is after doing?" I glanced towards the river and there was George heading back the way he'd come at a very fast walk. It was obvious he wasn't after a wounded bird as Belle, his yellow Labrador bitch, was by his side. He seemed to be heading for a small patch of gorse. The walk became a trot, finally he dropped his gun and ran. Danny's face was split with a grin from ear to ear.

"Didn't I say we'd have a great view? Wasn't Mr. Mac right when he said that black chocolate would give a man great energy."

I continued shooting. We were many gun shots apart so there was no worry about keeping in line. Shortly I heard shots to my right – George was back in action. We continued for some minutes and I had just managed a most pleasing right and left, when I heard Danny positively chortling with laughter. "My, he's a great mover so he is." I glanced towards the river. George was sprinting for another bush!

We continued on our way. Sport was excellent. Danny had been right when he had said it had been a good summer for snipe, for all we were seeing would be home bred birds. Meanwhile, out by the river, there was much action. George was noted for his energy for 'lacing' the ground – that is zigzagging so as to cover every ditch and every wet patch. However, he seemed to have developed a new technique, a quick dart from bush to bush, with the odd shot en route if a snipe happened to jump in his path. I was the first to reach the car. Bill was sitting on the bonnet gazing out across the callow. Jim joined us a few minutes later. Bill, with a deadpan face, remarked.

"Did you ever see the like? Isn't Mr. Mac the master man? Flitting from bush to bush. I'm telling you it were like watching a Jack Snipe so it was. No sooner was he up than he were down!"

George arrived about ten minutes later looking distinctly pale, swearing he'd got food poisoning. He was sure it was one of the sausages he'd had for breakfast! Fortunately, he seemed to have no further desire for black chocolate. At lunchtime, Jim did the decent thing and annexed it from the pocket of George's shooting coat and subsequently dropped it in the Shannon.

In spite of George's 'upset tummy', we had a wonderful day. The bag was a hundred and two snipe and twenty-three duck billed birds. As I left my friends to set out for Dublin I made Jim promise not to let George buy any more black chocolate from the chemist. Half way through the afternoon he had been complaining that he'd lost it and saying he must remember to replenish supplies that evening! He still claimed there was nothing like it to keep a man going.

CHAPTER 6

'Isn't diplomacy a great thing to be sure'

The winter passed quickly and, as the development of the estates progressed, so I found I had more and more weekends to myself to shoot or do whatever took my fancy. I even bought a horse, which I kept at Maynooth and managed a day's hunting most weeks, either with the North Kildare Harriers or the Ward Union. Provided I kept on top of my job I was virtually my own boss. However, I quickly learned that the Duke's slightest whim had to take precedence over all else. This, at times, led to disappointments, but such were the pleasures of life in Ireland that I learned to accept these and take them in my stride.

It was just at the end of the shooting season that I heard that Bryanstown, an adjoining property to the Maynooth estate, was up for sale. I hastily contacted the Chief Agent, George Ridley. Like me, he thought it could only be an asset and, after consultation with the Duke, gave me the go-ahead to buy it. There was what had been a delightful six bed roomed house, which the owner, who lived in Co. Meath, had vandalised. Part had been crudely divided into two workmen's cottages; whilst a hole had been knocked through the end of the drawing room wall and the latter, together with the dining room were being used as a machinery shed. Rough concrete steps had been built up the outside of the house leading up to the master bedroom which, together with the adjoining one, were currently used as an oat loft. In fact it was a mess! When I made my assessment of the property I gave little consideration to the house, the land was the main interest.

Just after contracts had been exchanged I was told I would have to find other accommodation at the latest by the end of the summer. Dartmouth Road was to be turned into flats. This was a real blow, for I had been very happy and comfortable there. It posed quite a problem too, as similar accommodation would be very hard to find. I mentioned this in passing to George Ridley, who was surprisingly non-committal. However, about a week later when I was at the London office he told me that he had been thinking about the question of where I should live and had decided I ought to live at Bryanstown. I protested that I couldn't possible afford to furnish, or, indeed, staff such an establishment. His reply was that no one was asking me to. He had talked to the Duke and the latter thought it was an excellent idea. The house would be furnished from the vast amount of furniture, surplus to requirements at Eaton Hall, the Duke's residence in Cheshire, that existed there since the army took over most of the Hall during the war. Further, a married couple would be employed to look after me. Who was I to argue?

The purchase was completed in time to carry out the Spring cultivations. Whilst walking round with Dick, planning the cropping and scheduling all the work to be done, I noticed several pheasants. A comparatively rare bird, except on the very limited number of keepered shoots in the country. Any shooting on the estate was mine and with two small coverts now included, I began to have visions of building up a small stock of pheasants. Except on shoots where they were hand reared, only cocks could be shot, hens were strictly taboo.

So keen was I on this idea that I purchased, with great difficulty and not a little expense, eight hen pheasants. These I penned close to the house before eventually releasing them. I recruited Tommy O'Neill, the herd who looked after the commercial cattle, to put out food for them several times a week. I spent a number of evenings, as soon as they were light enough, thinning out the vermin. All seemed to be going well with 'operation pheasant', particularly when, in due course, Tommy reported he'd seen three good broods. Two small fields, totalling some twelve acres, had been sown with mangolds, adjacent to Tommy's feed-ride, which provided excellent holding cover. Everything seemed set for an afternoon's pheasant shooting with my friends in November.

At the beginning of July I moved into Bryanstown. I had been fortunate in obtaining the services of an excellent couple, Charlie and Mrs. McManus. The latter explained that, as cook/housekeeper, she would expect to be addressed as such in keeping with her position! The garden was being completely remade, for it had become non-existent. To do this I had taken on 'Old Jim' Nolan. 'Young Jim' was already employed as the estate maintenance man. When I came out of the house after my first night in residence I was greeted by 'Old Jim' "Good day sorr an' did you hear himself?"

I enquired as to who 'himself' was and why I should hear him. Jim then launched into a long story. Apparently Bryanstown was haunted; supposedly by Colonel Lawless, who had built it at the end of the last century. Those who remembered the Colonel said he was most eccentric. A martinet of the highest order, who liked everything immaculate and drove his servants out of the house at 8.00 p.m. every night with a hunting whip! The staff lived in what were now the stables and accounted for something that had been puzzling me. Three of the loose boxes had chimneys on the top, but nothing inside. Obviously the grates and flues had long since been removed. According to Jim, the reason the main part of the house was converted into 'farm buildings' was because of 'himself' who made it impossible for anyone to live in that section. I laughed, thanked Jim for an interesting story and went on my way.

Several nights later I was reading in the drawing room at around 12.30 a.m. when I distinctly heard someone walking around in my bedroom overhead. My immediate reaction was that it could only be Charlie and what the devil did he think he was doing in my room! I shot up the stairs, at a rate that would have made it impossible for anyone to have got out of my room without my seeing them. It was empty. I went quietly along the corridor and listened outside the McManus' door. Rhythmic snoring assured me that both were in bed and asleep. Next day I was talking to Mrs. McManus and casually asked her if she had heard any rumours about Bryanstown being haunted? I was slightly concerned that she and Charlie might take fright if they believed the local gossip. "I have that. All nonsense so it is. Isn't there more to be feared from the living than the dead?" With that she dismissed the subject, much to my relief.

A week later I returned from Dublin quite late. I'd been schooling Spitfire, Harry Kellett's heavyweight hunter. I was going to show him for Harry at the Dublin Horse Show in August and had stayed on for supper and a chat. It was a warm July night and would have been really hot had it not been for quite a strong wind. I went up to my room. As I opened the door the curtains blew out from the open windows flapping in the breeze. I closed the door behind me. When I was about halfway across the room the door burst open, in spite of the strong wind blowing against it! Inwardly cursing the builders for not having hung the door properly I retraced my steps, closed it and checked that it was fastened. I had only just moved away from it when it flew open again. This was becoming monotonous. Again I closed it, but it only remained shut for seconds, but this time there was a difference. A hardbacked book, lying on the top of a chest of drawers just inside the door, went flying across the room!

Suddenly the penny dropped. I must be having a visitation from Colonel Lawless! I picked up the book, replaced it, closed and, this time, locked the door. I sat on the edge of the bed and considered the matter. There was no doubt that Mrs. McManus was right. Nevertheless it was an odd feeling, but not, I found, an alarming one. I decided I must have a chat to the ghostly Colonel. Feeling a bit of an idiot I cleared my throat and began. The gist of my conversation was that I knew how fond he had been of Bryanstown and how upset he must have become when it was so neglected. However, he had nothing more to worry about as, from now on, it would be well cared for, so would he please be a good chap and leave me in peace. I went downstairs and poured a whisky. Twenty minutes later I returned. The door remained closed and I had an excellent night's sleep. It seemed that the Colonel was happy, for, with one exception, I heard no more of him. The exception was after I was married, the night we returned from our honeymoon. There was much stomping around and banging of doors in the middle of the night. Fortunately Cynthia did not hear 'himself'. I slipped out of bed through to my dressing room and indulged in another little talk. It worked, that was the last I heard of the Colonel.

It was the second Saturday in October that I received a phone call from George. He was bored. It was most unusual for either of us to be at home at a weekend, but there was a most prestigious Ball being held in Dublin that night. Both Jim and George's wives had insisted on going. I was going with them accompanied by one of the many charming ladies I had met since moving to Ireland. Had it not been for this we would have been away at one of our favourite haunts in the West. George wanted to know if I would join him to shoot snipe locally for the remainder of the day. I readily agreed and suggested that he came out to me. We could start by shooting the Bryanstown marsh and then move on into Meath.

A little over half an hour later we set off, going out through the stable yard, where we met Tommy O'Neill. After a few minutes chat, Tommy asked if, in his capacity as honorary gamekeeper, he could accompany us. The answer was yes, and with Tommy walking between us we entered the marsh. It was full of snipe. George lived up to his reputation as the finest snipe shot in Ireland by pulling off three right and lefts. He only shot at six! I added a modest brace to the bag.

When we reached the end Tommy turned to me. "You remember O'Hara, the man we had the good white-head bullocks off a couple of weeks ago?"

"I do."

"Well, he has marshy fields too, so he has, away beyond Kilcock, just into Meath, acres of them. He told me you could bang away at the snipes any time. He says the place is crawling with them like chicken under yer feet an' terrible fat they are."

I looked at George and he nodded agreement. I doubted much of O'Hara's eulogy to Tommy, but then he was a cattle dealer, working in a world where everything was described with superlatives. Having picked up some sandwiches, which Mrs. McManus had prepared for us together with a couple of extra bottles of stout for Tommy, we were on our way. It must have taken a good thirty-five minutes to reach our destination, having negotiated a maze of by-roads and boreens. There by the gate, where Tommy told me to stop, was a car. My first thoughts were that somebody also knew of the marshy fields and had beaten us to it, but my fears were unfounded. It belonged to Paddy O'Hara. He was inspecting his cattle. These, fortunately, were up on the high ground so he had not been walking through the marsh disturbing the snipe. He greeted us warmly and was quick to tell me that he had a wagon of white-head bullocks the like of which could not be found if one travelled the length and breadth of Ireland for a month.

George, meanwhile, was scrutinising Paddy's dogs. "Queer little creature that one. It looks more like a fox that a dog."

"Sure now, an' aren't you right sorr. Isn't she out of me ole bitch here an' by a fox. That's the truth now." The old bitch was a typical brown working collie. Paddy continued. "I tethered herself out by th' wood, the big fox covert at the back of my house, when she were in season. Three nights I had her there. It'll be three years come the end of November. Dog foxes were barking all around each night, dozens of them there were. The rest of the time I had her locked away in a shed an' no dog got within an ass's roar of her. She had just one pup an' this is she."

I laughed." Paddy you can't cross a dog with a fox. Some dog must have got at her."

"I'm telling you, her da's a fox. Look at her colour, snipey nose, prick ears an' even a touch of a brush so she has. A grand wee cattle dog she is too. Just watch and see her run." He called her to him, then, waving an arm, sent her off. As she went up the field parallel to the hedge, her fast lope was that of a fox. At a hundred yards away she looked like a fox! Perhaps there was some substance to Paddy's claim. It is said that all things are possible! After arranging a time to see 'the greatest wagon of white-heads in Ireland', we set off.

Tommy told us that about half a mile to our right was a pond, a great place for duck. Soon we were there. After a hurried plan of campaign, George and I stationed ourselves behind two bushes, some forty yards apart. It was the only cover available. Tommy made a wide detour so as to approach the pond from the far side. We were in luck. A big flock of teal flew out between us. From our crossfire five came tumbling out of the sky. These were quickly retrieved by George's old labrador – Belle. We set off across the boggy fields, lacing them well and finding a good smattering of snipe, a number of which were going into our game bags. We must have gone about a mile when we came to a typical Land Commission bank. There seemed no reason for it to be there, unless at some time the Land Commission had thought about dividing the property into small holdings, decided the land was too wet and given up the idea.

George was the first to scramble to the top. As he reached it he called out 'golden plover' and leapt off the other side to take cover. A split second later, just as I reached the top, there was a startled yell and George came flying back in to view, arms and legs outstretched. I was in time to see he had landed on the back of a big stag, an outlier from the Ward Union. The startled beast had been lying under the bank when George had dropped onto him. Leaping up he catapulted George into the air, to land face down in the marsh. Tommy and I laughed so much that we couldn't go to my friend's assistance for several minutes. He staggered to his feet, slightly bemused, cursing volubly and dripping mud and water. He was soaked. Tommy positively hugged himself with glee. "Be the hokey, isn't Mr. Mac the great man? I'm telling you he's more laughs than the clown in Duffy's travelling circus so he is."

We decided to call it a day. It was the only time I knew George to say 'enough' when it was a matter of snipe shooting. However, it had

84

been an enjoyable part-day. We'd shot twenty-four snipe, five teal and four golden plover. We'd seen a fox-dog, or supposedly one and George, albeit for only a hundredth of a second, had ridden a stag. From that day on O'Hara's marshy fields were known as The Clown's Bog! That evening at the Ball, the day's events lost nothing in the telling as I recounted our adventures to Jim and Bobby Ganly.

The remainder of October passed quickly. The first of November, the start of the pheasant shooting season, was a Friday. I had arranged with Jim and George to join me for an early lunch on Saturday and then to walk the root crops and small coverts to see what sort of a stock of pheasants I had been able to rear. I left the office at around 2.00 p.m.. It was a gorgeous afternoon as I drove out of Dublin. My thoughts were on the morrow and wondering how much sport I would be able to show my friends. At least we should see enough to manage a brace of cocks each. Little enough, after all the wonderful shooting I had had with them.

I reached the end of the lane that led down to the entrance to Bryanstown, stopped before crossing the by-road and looked both ways. To my surprise, parked in the gateway into the first field of mangolds was a car. I drove the short distance up the road to investigate. As I got out I saw two men, plus a Pointer, hunting the mangolds. Seconds later a cock got up, a shot rang out and one of my precious pheasants collapsed. I was furious. Leaping into the car I raced off to the dairy farm where I knew Dick was waiting for me. Briefly I told him what was happening and sent him off to the Barracks in Maynooth to fetch a garda. I tore back, jumped out of the car and roared at the intruders. They looked round, ignored my shouting at them to come back onto the road and hurried on into the next field; whilst I overcame a desire to race after them.

It was only a matter of minutes before Dick's van pulled up and Garda Breen climbed out. He was a towering red-head from Co. Kerry. "Good day sorr. Is it the poachers you have?"

"It is garda. Two blaggards with a dog after my pheasants. They've shot at least one. I'm telling you, when we catch them, they're in serious trouble."

"'Tis true an' I'm thinking they'll no have a licence between them."

"Right garda, you stay here and catch them as they come out. We'll get round behind them and flush them out." Dick and I drove up to the house and set off across the fields. We had not gone far when we saw the two miscreants heading straight towards us. Alas, they too saw us and turned, heading back towards the road. We didn't hurry, knowing that Garda Breen was waiting. When we eventually came out onto the road, the latter was looking distinctly uneasy.

"Good man, you've got them then." On the ground lay three pheasants – one a hen! I nearly exploded with wrath. "Shooting hens are you? Well now you're really in trouble. I don't spend money on hen pheasants, trying to build up a stock to have the likes of you come and shoot them. Garda, throw the book at them." The two offenders glowered. One was about to say something when the Patrol Car drove up. Sergeant Donnelly, a really nice man who I knew well, climbed out.

"Hullo there sorr an' what's the trouble, poaching is it?"

"It is Sergeant and look – they've shot a hen. I want them charged on every possible count."

He glanced, for the first time, towards the two men. Suddenly his expression changed. As he moved towards them he started addressing them in Irish. He, like Garda Breen, started to look worried. After several minutes of earnest conversation, during which I was becoming more and more frustrated and annoyed, the sergeant returned to me, took me gently by the arm and walked me down the road out of hearing of the others. "We've a small wee problem so we have."

"I can't see any problem. We caught them red handed poaching my pheasants and, even worse, they've shot a hen. I want them brought to court."

"Whisht a while. 'Tis not so easy as you think. You see sorr they've been shooting here for years," He paused "An' well sorr, they're gardai from Dublin so they are. Two sergeants, like myself, coming up to the end of their time an' one a great friend of mine – a real decent man."

"So they may be, but they, of all people, should know better. If they didn't think they were in the wrong, why did they clear off when they saw Dick and me?"

The sergeant sighed. "You're a hard man so you are. Me friend is due for retirement in six months an' if you charge him he'll be reduced to the ranks, an' lose half his pension." He stood looking at me for what seemed like several minutes, as I weighed up the situation. It was difficult. I didn't want to get the wrong side of the sergeant.

As I pondered the matter, the sergeant spoke. "A man can make a mistake sorr, so he can. Tell me now, didn't I see you away across the fields, near Liam Connolly's, shooting last week?"

"Probably, but I don't see what that has to do with these two shooting my pheasants. Anyway I asked Liam and he said as far as he was concerned, I could shoot the marshes any time."

The sergeant smiled. "Isn't he the bold one, always codding. Sure now it'd be no concern of his how much you shot them. They're the Lord's marshes an' terrible fierce he can get if he hears a man's been poaching his land. But then, as I say, a man can easily make a mistake."

The inference of the sergeant's last remark was not lost on me. I thought quickly. His Lordship was our local Master of Hounds. I was dining with him that very evening and had been invited to his first day at the pheasants the following week. He had one of the best shoots in the country. I remembered Liam's grin when I asked him if I could shoot the marshes at the back of his farmyard and his reply. "Bang away, it'll no worry me." I had heard that he was a great joker. I wasn't sure that I liked being the butt for his humour. I also thought of all the wonderful shooting I enjoyed over other people's land, who never objected. True, poaching pheasants was rather different from shooting snipe but – what was good for the goose was good for the gander! "All right sergeant, I'll say no more about it, but only one condition."

"An' what is that?"

"That you, your friends and Garda Breen all come up to the house for a drink."

"We will that." The sergeant looked relieved as he shook me by the hand. We returned to the still glowering culprits. Sergeant Donnelly explained what we had decided. A look of relief spread across the faces of the two Dubliners. I was formally introduced and received firm handshakes. It was a new experience being introduced to poachers! After two very large Powers, the centre of the festivities left for Dublin, having, without being asked, deposited the pheasants in the hall. My magnanimity did not go so far as to say 'keep them'. Sergeant Donnelly showed no great desire to go. I poured him and Breen another drink and we chatted for about half an hour. The garda glanced at the clock on the mantle over the fireplace. "'Tis time I were off duty. 'Tis a good thing this week wasn't next week."

"How's that?"

"Well sorr, we'll be short staffed an' the barracks will be closed every Friday from 2.00 to 6.00 p.m."

"Oh! Well what happens if a major crime takes place at, say, ten past two? A murder for example."

Garda Breen thought about this before giving me his considered opinion. "Well sorr, I'm thinking that when we got there the body'd be stiff so it would!" I walked out to the car with Sergeant Donnelly. He shook my hand again.

"Thank you sorr, an' isn't the diplomacy a great thing to be sure!" With that he got into the car and drove away.

CHAPTER 7

'Tis terrible ghostly so it is'

It was not long after the incident of the pheasant shooting gardai, that I received a phone call early one Friday morning from Peter. The countryside, he said, around Oughterard was stiff with woodcock. Hard weather on the Continent and in Great Britain, had driven them to the more temperate clime of the West of Ireland. Peter was terribly anxious that I should motor across to Oughterard as soon as possible to shoot the next day, Saturday. His enthusiasm was infectious. He kept reiterating that the 'cock' could disappear just as quickly as they had appeared. For the last two evenings he had been sussing things out and there was a definite flight out across the lough, about three miles down the shore from his home. Whether they were going to some of the islands on Corrib or heading across the eleven miles of water for Cong, he did not know. The latter was an internationally famous woodcock shoot. Surprisingly, I had nothing special arranged for the weekend and, after only a moment's hesitation, I agreed. Peter was delighted and again assured me what a fantastic number of 'cock' there were in the area. He was sure my journey would not be wasted.

By the time I reached the Corrib Hotel it was getting late – nearly ten o'clock. Dinner, Derek assured me, was available if I would settle for smoked trout, followed by a fillet steak. I settled. Whilst my repast was being prepared I went through to the bar. It had been a long old drive on my own and I was very ready for a drink. Peter was waiting for me. I had never known him so excited. He'd been out again that evening. The 'cock' were still flighting, in even greater numbers than before. The moon was full and would be up almost as soon as it was dark. Conditions couldn't be better. Most of the activity seemed to be just after the moon rose and lasted, at the most, for a couple of hours. I absorbed this information as I sipped my Powers with enjoyment. I'd never flighted woodcock. It would be a novel and stimulating experience.

After my meal, which was excellent, I returned to the bar. I had no intention of having a late session, however many woodcock Peter had seen. We'd reserve that for the morrow, if successful. The company was much the same as when I went in for dinner except the little old man, Rory by name, who had been so enthralled by Ralph's account of shooting the rogue elephant had joined the party. He gave me a toothy grin.

"Good night sorr, an how's the helephant man? A real gentleman he was to be sure. He'd never see a man without a drink." I noticed Rory had no glass and rose, I hoped, to being classified as a 'real gentleman' by rectifying this. Peter told me his plans for the morning. Most of the 'cock' he'd seen were on the Galway side of Oughterard but he did not want to go over their holding ground during the day. He was anxious to leave it undisturbed for the evening flight. His plan was that we should try some really rugged country about four miles up towards the head of the lough. He had not been there to see if the 'cock' were equally plentiful in that area, but it was, he assured me, where he normally went when in search of woodcock.

The next morning it was dry with a strong southerly wind. The weather did not look too promising, but as long as the wind continued we were unlikely to be troubled by rain. We quickly arrived at our destination, parked the car and set off. Peter had not been exaggerating when he had described the country we were to cross as rugged. It was similar to that which we had walked for 'cock' when Ralph had been with us, only worse! It was impossible to keep to a straight line because of the boulders, clumps of hazel and scrub. Apart from the difficulty of actually negotiating the terrain, it was a constant worry for both Peter and myself knowing where the other was. Literally scrambling along for most of the time, it was not easy to shoot with any great accuracy.

During the morning we must have put up between twenty five and thirty woodcock. Due to the terrible conditions under foot, less than half of these were shot at. We walked in a circle and arrived back at the car just after noon, very ready for a much needed drink and some food. The bag was not impressive – six, but as Peter said – more than we would have shot sitting in the hotel waiting for the evening flight! After a rest, I drove on another mile or so and once more we set off across similar terrain. The going was not quite as hard, but hard enough. We did not see many 'cock', in fact we walked for nearly an hour without the sign of one. By half three I'd had enough. I was scratched, stiff and sore! Peter raised no objection when I said enough was enough. We had added three more to the bag.

We returned to the hotel and sat in front of a roaring fire, eating hot buttered toast and drinking tea. The wind had dropped and it had all the makings of a clear bright evening. Peter said he thought we ought to be in position soon after six. The moon, he estimated, would be up by half past. With some reluctance I left the comfort of the hotel and set off through a maze of boreens that bounded the lough. Peter told me we could drive within a few hundred yards of where we wanted to go and could park in O'Rourke's yard.

We were getting our guns out of the back of the car when the cottage door opened and Mrs O'Rourke appeared. "Good night men. Oh, 'tis you Peter. I thought it were someone bringing my Paddy back. He's away to the fair at Maam's Cross an' drunk he'll be when he returns."

"We're just off, Mary, to the three big rocks, close to the water's edge to flight 'cock'. We'll be about a couple of hours, so you'll know who it is when we return."

"Go down there is it? I'm telling you Peter, I'd not set foot near that place after dark." She crossed herself. "'Tis terrible ghostly so it is. Even in daylight it sends the shivers down me spine. Take care men." With that she went back into the house.

By the time we'd reached the end of the boreen the moon was starting to rise. I could see that all around us was scrub and boulder, similar to that which we'd been walking all day. The lane opened out into a rough grassy field, dotted with great lumps of granite that ran down to the waters edge some seventy to eighty yards away. Peter took me to a place where there were three large rocks close together; about thirty yards back from the cover.

"You stay here. I'll go on for about three hundred yards to another big rock, so you can shoot anywhere quite safely. There will be nobody else around."

I took up my position behind one of the boulders and glanced at my watch. It was nearly half six and the moon was rising fast. Some green plover flew over, they showed up clearly and it would have been no problem to have taken a shot at them. The adrenalin flowed, as I scanned the edge of the scrub in hopeful anticipation. Would the 'cock' flight tonight, or had they moved on to the other side of the lough? My thoughts were rudely interrupted by a voice immediately behind me. I nearly jumped out of my skin. So much for Peter's "there will be nobody else around".

"Good night sorr. Is it the 'cock' yer after? You're only just in time. They'll all be gone this night so they will."

"It is, and you gave me a terrible start coming up behind me like that. I never heard a sound."

My companion chuckled. "Sure, an' why should you?"

I turned and took a quick look at my visitor. The moon was up and it was as bright as could be. He was tall, thin faced and was wearing a suit of coarse tweed, probably a home weave, muffler and a very old billy-cock hat. I really didn't want anyone standing with me, but, for all I knew, he could be the owner of the field.

"Do you live locally and would you mind standing in under one of the rock, so you won't be seen?"

"Well now in a manner of speaking you could say that. The 'cock' will take no notice of me. Anyhow you'll see none for ten minutes or so."

"Really." I kept scanning the skyline, but saw nothing. I could sense my visitor was still with me. I wished he'd go away, he made me feel uneasy. After some minutes he suddenly spoke.

"To yer right sorr, to yer right. There'll be two any second now. Get ready, for they'll not be waiting on you."

Suddenly I saw the unmistakable silhouette of a woodcock. I raised my gun, swung on it and fired and saw it crumple. A second came into view, flying almost the same line. I fired again, that too was down. "Good man yerself. You has them both, so you has."

"Great!" I turned smiling to my uninvited companion. "I'll want you as a witness, so I can claim by bottle of Bols gin. What's your name?"

"Sean Byrne. Is it the gin you gets now for shooting a couple of ole 'cock?"

"It is. Now keep quiet please, there could easily be more coming."

I glanced round. There was no one there. I could see for several hundred yards around me. It was totally impossible for anyone to have moved that quickly. He'd spoken to me only seconds before I turned round. Sean Byrne had come and gone without a sound. It was positively eerie. I heard Peter getting some shooting and managed to bag two more myself. I missed more than I am prepared to say – it was very tricky shooting. About eight o'clock Peter joined me. He had a brace, but had had nothing like as much shooting as I had. His old spaniel quickly collected my birds and we headed back to the car.

On the way I told Peter about Sean Byrne. "Strange, I've never heard of him. I'll make some enquiries tomorrow and when I find him, I'll get something in writing that he saw you shoot a right and left of woodcock."

I dropped Peter off at his home on my way back to the hotel. He said he'd see me around ten o'clock. I felt I was in for a late night, but so what? It had been a great day. Fifteen woodcock was something of which to be proud. After dinner I went through to the bar. Peter was already there. We wet the heads of my right and left of 'cock' in no uncertain manner. Being a Saturday night, Derek made sure the bar closed at midnight. That, probably, was a good thing. Rory was in particularly good form but couldn't make up his mind which was the greater achievement "to shoot a helephant or down two of them ole 'cocks'.

I left early the next morning without seeing Peter. In fact I never saw a soul as I drove out of Oughterard. That night Peter telephoned me. He had made extensive enquiries, but no one knew a Sean Byrne. However, he learned from one of the elders that there had been a man of that name living where the O'Rourkes did now. He had died at least 60 years ago. According to Peter's informant he'd been a great shooting man and was well known for the hard wearing tweed that he used to weave. Peter went on to tell me that he had spent a couple of hours at the three rocks, where I had been the night before. He hadn't seen a woodcock – they'd gone! As I put the phone down I had a most strange feeling, really spooky. Mary O'Rourke's words came flooding back to me. Could it have been.........? Well, I'd never know, but now it seemed most unlikely I'd get my bottle of Bols!

Earlier in the year, I had been assisting at the Fitzwilliam Lawn Tennis Club during Tournament week. It was Ireland's leading event in this sphere, held the week immediately following Wimbledon. I was only a 'bar member', but had been co-opted onto the committee to help deal with organising the spectators. About halfway through the week I had gone into the bar one evening. There I found Jim Ganly talking to a most attractive girl. He called me across and introduced us. Her name was Cynthia Goodbody. A surname, which, in due course, was to lead to much ribaldry from several of my friends on the Westminster staff.

Not only was Cynthia extremely easy on the eye and a good conversationalist, but she was, by Irish standards, a first class tennis player. I also learned that she was an airhostess with Aer Lingus. Jim left us and after watching an excellent men's singles, or, to be precise, the final set, we went to the Russell Hotel for dinner. This had recently been described by the Duke, much to the amusement of the owner, whom I knew well, as 'the best little café in Europe'. That had been in early July.

The week after I returned from 'cock' shooting at Oughterard, I was checking in for a flight to London when I heard a voice behind me. "Hello Michael. Where are you off to?" It was Cynthia, looking most attractive in her uniform. She was, she told me, just going out on a plane to Glasgow. However, it appeared that she had a few minutes for a chat. The outcome of which was that I arranged to take her out to dinner the following Thursday evening. It had been most enjoyable. One meeting led to another and my bog-trotting friends raised eyebrows and gave knowing looks at each other, particularly when I opted out of a morning duck flight as I was taking Cynthia out the night before.

However, I did say I would be at the hotel in Banagher in time for breakfast to shoot snipe for the remainder of the day. Amongst her many attributes I discovered that Cynthia was keen on shooting. Further, she had a Golden Retriever, Dave, whom she assured me was trained as a gundog. He had a magnificent pedigree coming from one of England's leading kennels, the heart of a lion and was destined to be the first Golden Retriever dog to become a champion in Ireland.

Dave had spent several months with a part time trainer, living on the banks of the Shannon. The following season Cynthia had regularly worked him on a snipe shoot close to her home and had even managed to get several days picking up on one of the very few pheasant shoots in the country. Work had then taken Cynthia to England and Dave had remained at home with her family, none of whom shot. They were all keen followers of rugby football and played cricket and tennis. However, her father was dog mad and a complete 'push over' for Dave! In no time at all he was swinging on the end of a walking stick, had stones thrown for him to retrieve and lumps of wood being hurled into rivers and lakes for his amusement. He was an incredible swimmer and would sooner be in water than on dry land.

When Cynthia joined Aer Lingus she had little thought of ever working Dave again. Even with her limited knowledge she realised what her father was doing with her dog was quite contrary to what any gundog should be allowed to do. I heard of all Dave's exploits; of the time, on the Shannon, when a pike had taken a snipe, just as he had his mouth open to retrieve it; how he would jump nine feet off a bridge into a river to collect a dummy, a feat I subsequently witnessed on a number of occasions and of his ability to carry eggs without ever cracking one. But all this had been before Cynthia had gone to England.

So much Irish charm, plus a paragon of a gundog were enough to make any man feel 'broody'. I began to have definite thoughts that perhaps Bryanstown could accommodate two as easily as one! Cynthia had not seen my home and I felt it time that she did. Sunday lunch was arranged and Dave was to come too. In the afternoon it was planned that we should take a walk out into the marsh and shoot a few snipe for Dave's entertainment. This would allow Cynthia to show off his prowess for, in spite of it being nearly two seasons since he had worked, she felt he had lost none of his ability.

Mrs. McManus really rose to the occasion. I opened a rather special bottle of wine and by the time we retired to the drawing room for coffee I felt more like staying in front of the fire than facing what, in Ireland, is known as a 'soft' afternoon. That meant that it was bucketing rain! I pointed out that it wasn't really the kind of weather to go wandering around a marsh and that we'd be far better off in the dry and warm, but it was no good. Cynthia was dead keen to show me how well Dave could work. I, by then, was dead keen to please Cynthia; so somewhat grudgingly, I got my gun and we donned our waterproofs. As we reached the gate into the field that we had to cross to get to the marsh, we met Tommy. I enquired as to why he was out at that time on a Sunday afternoon? He explained that there was a bullock in Marsh Field he thought wasn't looking just right that morning and he was off to take another look at it. I told him I was going to shoot snipe, so he'd better come along with us and wait to look at the bullock until I'd shot the marsh.

Dave made a passably good job at walking to heel, considering he'd not been asked to for so long. Tommy eyed him with the shrewd awareness of a man who knows good livestock.

"Isn't he the great one."

Cynthia smiled happily. "Yes, he's only to win two more points to become the first Champion of his breed in the country. That is once he's got his Working Certificate."

"Is that so? Well I'm thinking that'll be no trouble to a boyo like him."

We were nearing the gate into the marsh. I signalled for quiet. I whispered to Cynthia to put Dave on a lead. I didn't want to risk him galloping off as soon as I fired a shot. Tommy opened the gate to let us through and, leaning on it, took up his position to watch the sport. We hadn't advanced more than about twenty yards when a snipe jumped, in front and to the right. As I fired another appeared to the left. I squeezed the trigger again. That too was down. A right and left. The look of admiration on Cynthia's face did my ego no harm at all!

I moved over to Cynthia and told her to send Dave for whichever one she liked. She slipped off his lead and he was gone like a bullet straight to the first one. No hesitation, a spot on mark. This was some dog! Then to my surprise, instead of coming back, he made a bee line for the second. Again he knew exactly where it was and, gathering it up, returned at speed to his smiling mistress with the two. It was only as he came towards us that I realised that there was something flying out from either side of his mouth. To begin with I thought he had picked up a length of old binder twine in his haste, then I realised to my horror, it was the snipe's guts. He handed over his mangled offering to Cynthia with great joy. She took it, turned and passed it to me. Not a word was said, as tears ran down her cheeks. I headed for the gate, there was no point in going on for, thanks to Cynthia's father, Dave had developed a mouth like a rat trap!

As Tommy greeted us, a broad smile spread across his face. "Be the hokey an' hasn't he the eye. With the streamers an' all you'd be thinking you were at a carnival so you would." With that he went off to look at the bullock. We walked in silence back towards the house. Then I started to laugh, well it was no good crying! I put my arm around Cynthia's shoulder and pulled her towards me, it was still bucketing with rain. We were married the following August. That's more than five decades ago. Since that day we've had many good Goldens, winners on the bench and in the field, but we've never had another Dave, who proved without any shadow of doubt that retrieving snipe and stones don't mix!

CHAPTER 8

'Micky's fox'

Marrying Cynthia, I discovered, was, amongst many other things, an introduction into the world of pedigree gundogs. In no time at all the Bryanstown kennel of Golden Retrievers was formed. As part of my wedding present to Cynthia, a trip was arranged to England, to buy the best young bitch she could obtain, a future bride for Dave. She was most fortunate in being able to purchase a really outstanding young bitch from one of the leading dual-purpose kennels. This was the start of a hobby that has lasted over fifty years and which has involved us both.

Cynthia received another four-legged wedding present – a superb, if aged, hunter from a cousin, Betty Draper, wife of the famous trainer Tom. The mare, Drenagh, was a noted performer with the Ward Union. However, her owner felt the gruelling long gallops across Co. Meath was asking too much of this big-hearted mare. She was eighteen, and would have literally galloped herself into the ground had she been allowed. So her owner decided to pass Drenagh on to where she knew her beloved old mare would be cherished and cared for. Further, that the latter would still be able to get out with hounds. Our local pack was the North Kildare Harriers, a lot of fun, but much less demanding on a horse than the staghounds. It was obvious that hunting was lifeblood to Drenagh, the sight or sound of hounds totally rejuvenated her! She made sure that her new mistress was always in the van of any hunt in which she participated. Alas, I was not able to get out hunting as often as I would have liked. Consequently, I became less fit and was not able to ride with quite the force and determination I found so exhilarating. However, I persevered and puffed.

My circle of friends and acquaintances around Ireland had increased and multiplied rapidly. This resulted in my having a number of 'ports of call' as I travelled the country, this in turn lead to my hunting with a variety of packs, other than our local ones. Frequently this would be to try a horse with a view to buying it. It could be for the Duke himself, or indeed as a present for one of his friends; or it might be for one of my chums in England. The price in Ireland, in those days, would probably be less than half what a similar mount would cost in

England. It was when looking for a horse for a friend of the Duke's that I first met John Joseph O'Keefe, known to his friends as J.J. I regularly passed his establishment, but seldom without calling.

It was the beginning of March that I pulled up in front of O'Keefe's and got out of my car. I entered and made my way through the shop, running the gauntlet of half sides of bacon, hurricane lanterns, rubber boots and a host of other goods that hung from the low ceiling, impeding one's progress to the bar. O'Keefe's was typical of hundreds of stores throughout rural Ireland during the forties and fifties, that could supply anything from a tin tack to a ton of fertilizer. J.J.'s however was different. For in addition, at the rear of the premises he ran two other businesses, an undertakers and a thriving horse dealership. There did not seem to be any demarcation as to where one ended and the other began. On one occasion I had looked into a loosebox and there, neatly stacked on a well strawed floor were eight coffins!

I entered the bar and found J.J. behind the counter deep in conversation with Dan O'Rafferty, the hunt's earth stopper and Micky Hughes, a keen hunting farmer.

"Good night sorr, 'tis grand to see you an' well yer looking." J.J. shook me warmly by the hand, as did the others. I ordered drinks all round, lit my pipe and settled down on a bench by the smoking turf fire.

"Well, any news? It seemed to me when I came in that you three were plotting something." They grinned sheepishly at one another.

"We might have been an' again we might not. Dan, Micky, shall we tell him? After all hasn't he proved many a time how he enjoys a bit o' sport." John Joseph looked at his two companions. They nodded and put their empty glasses down. J.J. filled them without a word and poured me another Powers.

Then he cleared his throat. "Well now, you know the Captain is giving up the hounds at the end of the season. A nice poor man if ever there was one, with not a bad thought in his head, but if it weren't for Luke (the first whipper-in and kennel huntsman) never a fox would he catch. Well Micky, Dan an' I've been thinking that 'himself' should have a hunt to remember three weeks tomorrow, that's the Tuesday, his last day as Master. Hounds'll meet here at th' top end of the street. Now, if you'll swear never to breathe a word, I'll be telling you how it can be done." I swore. "Well now th' Master'll be drawing Micky's gorse first. As you know, Micky always goes away to the bottom side to keep watch. Well he's after tellin' me that there's not a smell of a fox above at his place. So not wantin' to disappoint 'himself', it being his last day an' all, we're thinking of laying a class o' line at night. Terrible strong stuff it'll be." He took a swig of his porter and continued. "We thought we'd run across to the big rough field at the back of the creamery without a break. That's a good four miles so it is, give the dogs a bit of a breather an' then head away across the river. Micky's brother Ben has a wee farm up on the hill beyond. After a few minutes, Ben'll hold his cap up an' holler blue murder. We'll take the dogs away for another five or six miles, giving them a couple of checks an' then make out th' varmints gone to ground. It'll be in the next hunt's country, so 'himself' can't dig. What do you think?" I wished they hadn't told me, for at heart I'm a bit of a purist.

"I'll tell you what I think. I don't think I ever heard this conversation. I'll say no more." I bought another round of drinks and in due course was about to take my leave when J.J. spoke up.

"I have a grand young horse coming in, leaps like a stag so he does. He's yours for the last day of the season, if you can spare the time." It was a tempting offer and I was intrigued to know how the day would go. So, subject to not being tied up with some unexpected work I accepted the mount.

Three weeks later, astride a really good sort of middleweight hunter, I made my way from O'Keefe's to the meet at the far end of the street. There was a great turn out of followers and I saw that the Masters from the two adjoining hunts were present to help give the Captain a really good send off. There was much drinking and toasting the Master, the latter very much entering into the spirit of the occasion. I rode up to him. He greeted me warmly and said how good it was of me to come to his last meet and he hoped he would be able to show good sport. As he said that, Dan O'Rafferty passed behind him and, much to my embarrassment, gave me a conspiratorial wink. I moved away, although it was difficult, for the street was packed with horses and riders. I saw people I knew from the Ward and then to my surprise and delight Father Pat. He greeted me like a long lost brother.

I enquired as to what brought him to that neck of the woods. "Hunting, what else? Haven't I a cousin, deals a bit in horses, only a few miles from here an' me back at Maynooth for a week. Wasn't it the only thing I could do, but come and see the Captain off"? He eyed my mount. "My but that's a great sort, so it is. I'm thinking my cousin would give you fifty pounds for him." I laughed.

"I'm sure he would, but he's one of O'Keefe's." At that moment we were joined by J.J., riding the ugliest horse I ever laid eyes on. I had in fact seen him before, but equally, he was one of the best performers I have ever seen across country. He was the only horse John Joseph ever owned that he would not sell. He had bought St. Patrick, as he became known, off the tinkers for a tenner. He had been skin and bone and J.J. told me, he was so weak that he had great difficulty in getting the poor creature back to his stables, only three miles away.

The master blew his horn and, with Luke clearing a way through the crowd, headed for Micky's gorse. I was flanked by J.J. and Father Pat. The former tapped me on the knee with his whip. "You needn't be affeared to have a go on that boyo. I'm telling you he's no ordinary yoke. He'd clear the Styx if you asked him." We reached Micky's farm and rode through the yard, scattering the hens and ducks as we went.

The owner came up to the Master, we were right behind him. "Shall I away to the bottom Captain, to view the varmint if he heads up the valley? I've one for you Master, or as sure as any man can be. Terrible big he is an' as bold as ole Nick himself. Why, didn't he take one of my Mary's hens only the other night and her not twenty yards away."

"Thank you Micky, I'd be obliged."

We waited for our farmer host to canter off out of sight to the bottom side of some five or six acres of gorse. I looked round the field, as I checked the girths. There must have been eighty or ninety followers. Any time I'd been out with the Captain before, there had only been thirty to forty in the field at the most. After a few minutes calling his hounds, the Master rode forward and put them into cover. We waited expectantly. Suddenly a hound whimpered, the Captain encouraged them, then another joined in. This was followed by an ear splitting view halloo from Micky. Doubling on his horn the Master galloped down the side of the gorse, whilst Luke rated any laggards left behind. The three of us, as close to the Captain as etiquette would allow, rounded the corner.

Micky was there, hat aloft, still hollering, hounds streaming away at breath taking speed. I glanced behind me, it seemed we'd got a 'flyer'. The first big bank loomed ahead. I saw Father Pat's horse land on the face of it, before scrambling to the top. It was obviously more experienced than his mount the day we first met with the Ward. Mine gathered his hocks under him and launched himself into the air with the agility of a gazelle. He balanced on the top before leaping out over something that looked like an arm of the sea! J.J. had been right, this was no mean performer.

Hounds streamed away, giving tongue, sweet music, but the secret that I felt I had partially nurtured, gave me a sense of guilt. But there was no time for recriminations, bank after bank rose before us as we sped across the countryside. I galloped level with the Captain across one field. There was a look of such sheer joy on his face that I felt the conspirators were nearly justified. I could see the creamery chimney about half a mile ahead and, as my mount pecked badly on landing, nearly shooting me out of the front door, I thought of the now much needed breather that both horses and riders were about to get.

Again I was level with the Master. He turned to me, his face alight with pleasure, eyes sparkling. "What a scent, what a scent. Did you ever hear such music? What a pack. Hell, I'll miss them." I saw tears running down his face, as we bore down on the next bank. Seconds later, hounds lifted their heads. The Master rode forward to cast them. I jumped off my horse and loosened the girths, as did Father Pat. The latter, grinning from ear to ear, offered me his flask. I hesitated. "Don't make strange, it'll not harm you. There's a drop of Tullamore Dew in it, the best of Irish whiskeys."

Gratefully I took a swig. I looked at J.J. He was still walking St. Patrick round. I remained on the ground. I felt it would be time enough to remount when my friend decided to. It was a good five minutes at least before we heard a far off holloa. There, on the hill, about half a mile away, I could just make out a figure holding up his hat. Calling hounds the Captain galloped off. The fun continued to be great, but not quite so fast. As we reached higher and more stony land, so the obstacles began to vary. Stone walls started to replace banks and those, thank goodness, that we did meet were not as terrifyingly tall as in the vale. Hounds checked again. Micky, who was right up with the Master, turned to the Captain. "Shall I gallop on an' see if I can get a view of the varmint?"

"Do Micky, do. It would be a shame to lose him now." Micky rode off and, about three small fields away, stopped, held up his hat and gave an ear splitting holloa. The Master gathered up his hounds which were spread across the field, and cantered off. It was easy to see that both horse and rider had nearly had enough.

"Along the bottom bank Master." Micky pointed to the far end of the field. "I'm tellin' you he's near done, so he is." The Captain cast hounds. Again they hit the line and sweet music filled the air, but not for long. Two fields further on they suddenly stopped, baying and scratching at a hole that lead into what was obviously a very large badgers' set. It stretched for many yards along the face of the hill. The Master jumped off his horse and blew 'to ground'. As I dismounted I looked around me. There were not many finishers; I counted fifteen as well as J.J. and myself. I noticed the two neighbouring MFHs, a well known thruster from the Ward, but no Father Pat. I was wondering what could have happened to him, when J.J. gave me a poke in the back with his hunting crop and gestured towards the Master. "I'm telling you that's one happy man. Nine miles as the dogs ran. 'Tis the greatest hunt he ever had an' I'm thinking he'll remember this day to his death."

As he said this Father Pat rode into sight. Quickly I saw that his breeches were smothered in mud. When he reached us he dismounted. I looked him up and down and then, smilingly enquired. "Hallo, what happened to you? Did you get off to say a prayer?"

The holy father gave me a withering look. "Aren't you the funny one? But I'm thinking I'll have a few prayers to say tonight, to make up for what I called this yoke when he came down at that last bank."

The Master and Luke brought hounds back from the hole. The former then walked over to Father Pat, J.J. and me. "What a hunt! One I'll always remember. Never remember a better scenting day. Marvellous, marvellous!" Father Pat pulled out his flask and, raising it towards the Master, took a good swig before passing it round. It was empty by the time it got back to him.

"We better not let the horses get chilled. Mount up boys, we've a long hack home." As Father Pat said this he turned to me and put his arm around my shoulder. "Well me ould segotia, aren't you glad you came to Ireland?" I assured him I was. It had been a fantastic hunt, but secretly I did so wish I had known nothing about Micky's 'fox'.

It was indeed a long hack back, but the time passed quickly in the company of J.J., Micky and my clerical friend. To add to the interest I had decided to buy my mount from John Joseph. The haggling over the price occupied a number of miles and my two companions gave much help. At last a deal was agreed – one hundred pounds. Then came the question of the luck penny. By the time this had been agreed, five pounds, we were nearly back at J.J's yard! I sent my purchase to a friend in England where he quickly became a star performer in one of the most fashionable counties.

Several weeks later I was passing J.J's and as usual called in. The bar was empty except for 'himself' and Sean Duffy, a strong supporter of the local pack of Beagles. I had met the latter before and soon we were deep in conversation. Apparently 'them little hare dogs' as J.J. called them, had a fantastic hunt, the Saturday after the Captain's farewell meet. The first draw had been the rough field behind the creamery. Hounds had owned a line almost at once. None of the followers had seen a hare go away, but the pack had gone screaming off. So fast, Sean assured me, that no man living could have stayed with them. Eventually, after much searching, they had caught up with the hounds just below Micky Hughes' gorse! J.J. gave me a wink as he topped up my glass. "I'm telling you, that must have been a terrible strong scent to make them little dogs run like that. A man could be forgiven in thinking they were chasing an old fox!"

John Joseph took me off to see 'The greatest four year old you ever laid an eye on'. There was no doubt about it, it was a top quality horse. A brown gelding with a white blaze and one white sock, beautifully constructed and, as J.J. said, 'had a lep in him like a stag, so he had.' After getting some idea as to what price would secure this equine masterpiece, I headed back for Bryanstown, having first phoned Cynthia to say I'd be half an hour late for dinner.

Spring quickly turned to summer. This, I was to find led to a weekly round, when weather permitted, of tennis parties. The social life in rural Ireland was very much what it had been in England between the wars. Cynthia was much in demand, her prowess on the courts being well known. These weekend parties were real fun events and through them I became acquainted with a lot of interesting and charming people. Amongst these was Barbara Eustace-Duckett MFH. I had been introduced to her at Lady Brooke's. An invitation to one of her tennis parties was akin to a royal command. She was a lady of considerable charm, but an undoubted autocrat. The first time I attended one of her tennis afternoons, I immediately detected a certain nervous undercurrent amongst the male members of the party. I did not give the matter much thought until I learned that I had been chosen to partner our hostess, against Cynthia and the male star of the North Kildare tennis circuit!

As I prepared for the fray, several of my men friends wished me luck, including Patrick Ellis. He was even a bigger rabbit on the tennis court that I was. The Ellis family had moved from Yorkshire to the nearby Straffen House estate just around the time I had moved into Bryanstown. Molly Ellis, Patrick's mother, owned one of the leading herds of Jersey cattle in England and had transported them en bloc to Ireland. We had become close friends, for apart from our interests in agriculture, Patrick was a keen hunting and shooting man. He managed the estate, and under his guidance, an excellent keepered pheasant shoot was being developed. As I picked up my racquet, about to do battle, he put his hand on my shoulder and said, "I hope you're fit and have your running shoes on."

I thought his comment was because of the tough opposition, for it had quickly become apparent, to those who had seen me perform with both gun and racquet, that I was very definitely more at home with the former. The male pairing for the foursome was undoubtedly wrong, it should have been the other way round. On instructions from our hostess, Cynthia spun a racquet. Lady Brooke called 'smooth'. It was 'rough'. Picking up two balls, my partner declared we would serve and retired to the base line, from whence she delivered some really sneaky underarm serves!

Lady B. was of ample proportions. The moment she had sent the ball on its way, she advanced with quite amazing alacrity to the service line, straddling it at the junction with the centre line. There she steadfastly remained, legs planted firmly apart, brandishing her racquet and shouting "Run boy, run" until the rally was over. Her mode of address, I was to discover later, applied equally to a retired admiral, who surely had no change out of his three score years and ten, as it did to me. It proved to be the most arduous game of tennis in which I was ever involved! I ran frantically round my hostess. Cynthia, I could see, was nearly convulsed with suppressed laughter.

Both she and her partner were obviously knocking back 'dollies', just to make me sprint around the court. The climax of the match came when Cynthia lobbed her ladyship. The ball landed immediately behind her, this was accompanied by the now familiar cry of "Run boy, run". Pantingly, I responded and pulled off the tennis shot of my life. A running backhand that passed between the aristocratic legs hit the top of the net and rolled over for the point!

It would not have "been the thing" for Cynthia and her partner to have defeated their hostess too convincingly. We were allowed to take four games. To me it was obvious that the opposition was slowly sending the ball first left, then right, so that I had no option but to try for every one! It nearly killed me circumnavigating her ladyship. When we came off the court I was drenched with sweat; my partner didn't even glow! However, she turned to me and said, "Thank you, but if only you'd run we could have won that."

I went off to change my shirt, after partaking of several glasses of ice-cold lemonade. I was making my way back to the centre of the afternoon's entertainment, when I came face to face with a rather stern looking lady, that was until she smiled. From her dress it was obvious that she had no intention of participating in anything more energetic than a walk around the garden. She greeted me warmly. "Just the man I want to talk to. I'm Barbara Eustace-Duckett, we were introduced earlier. Did you enjoy partnering Rosey?" There was a look in her eye that gave me the feeling that I could be honest. My reply was monosyllabic.

"No."

She laughed.

"Come and sit in the shade and talk." She was, I knew, the doyen of the Labrador Retriever world in Ireland. Apparently she had been hearing about Cynthia's and, to a lesser degree, my activities in starting up a Golden Retriever Club in Ireland. She felt we should get together over a number of matters of mutual interest, particularly field trials. We found we had much in common and that afternoon was the start of many years of friendship. Eventually we made our way back to the courts, just in time to see Cynthia finishing a match, partnering our hostess. The latter had taken up her normal position, but the cry had changed. It was now "good girl" as Cynthia cut every return off at the net, winning point after point. We all went in for tea, our hostess elated by a six love win! Over a really superb repast, I introduced

Cynthia to Barbara and before we parted later in the evening, it was agreed that she would contact us before long about field trials.

It was not until the middle of October that I heard from Barbara. She 'phoned late one evening to tell me she required me to steward at a field trial. It wasn't so much a request as a command. She was a delightful lady, but used to having entirely her own way when it came to anything to do with gundogs. Apparently the Trial was being held at The Knockdrin Castle estate, the home of the Dunne Cullinans, good friends of Cynthia's and her parents. In fact Paddy Dunne Cullinan was the first person to bring a bitch to Dave. I enquired why it was so important that I should steward?

"Because you are a keen shooting man and involved in dogs. I shall probably need you as a judge before long, and I want to see how you shape up. Apart from stewarding, keep notes, make your own assessments. I shall question you afterwards."

There was no Irish Kennel Club panel of field trial judges in those days. Professional trainers were a rarity and 'handling', as we know it today, was conspicuous by its absence. Never-the-less, the top dogs attained a very high standard of game finding ability, frequently under very tough conditions. Already judging a variety of farm livestock, plus hunters and ponies, I did not find the prospect of judging at a Trial in any way daunting.

Three weeks later Cynthia and I arrived at Knockdrin in time to join the owners for a cup of coffee, as they were finishing their breakfast. Barbara had been staying overnight at the Castle. As secretary (for which really one should read dictator, in the nicest possible sense) of the Labrador Retriever Club of Ireland, Barbara would be in charge of the day's event. Cynthia was told that she was to assist. In due course we emerged onto the drive to meet judges, guns and competitors.

There was a great air of bonhomie. Everyone knew everyone present, except one or two of the guns. These were quickly introduced. One whom I had not met, was an Honourable (subsequently to inherit an Earldom). Whilst I had not met him before, I had heard some hair-raising accounts of his rather abandoned ways with a gun in the shooting field!

The lady for whom I was to steward, I had met twice before. She bred Irish Water Spaniels, had great charm and could be described as 'twittery'. I discovered it was her first judging appointment, outside of her own breed. She was scared stiff! We, I was told, would be on the right of the line, covering guns one to four. 'The Honourable' was number one. A fact that did nothing to enhance my morning, particularly when our host had given himself number eight! As we lined out to start the Trial I was quickly convinced that the stories I had heard about 'The Honourable' were not without foundation. I have a distinct aversion to looking down the wrong end of the barrels, even when I know the gun is empty.

I called our first two dogs into line. Number two was owned by Willie MacDougald, a veterinary surgeon, whom I knew well. He was a great friend of the Ganlys and we had shot together a number of times at Banagher. I knew his bitch Sally too and after a lifetime of shooting and some fifty years judging field trials in a number of countries, I consider her the best game finder I ever saw. The estate, like so many in Ireland, was encircled by a wall. We started out with the extreme right of the line adjacent to this. It ran parallel to a road. At a command from Barbara the line moved forward. We advanced through fairly open woodland, but with plenty of ground cover in the way of briars and bracken. It was not many minutes before two woodcock jumped, well within the range of 'The Honourable'. He downed the first, swung on the second as it climbed high and fast over the demesne wall and fired again. 'The Honourable' gave a shout of "right and left of cock", but he was nearly drowned out by a yell, bordering on a scream, followed by a loud thud. Where we were, due to the undulation of the ground, it was just possible to peer over the wall.

One of the beaters took a look. He called out to his nearest companion. "Jasus, hasn't himself bagged a Post Office linesman, as well as the 'cock'." Then he turned and called across to 'The Honourable'. "Youse a man killed so you have an' terrible vexed he is too!"

"Nonsense, what's the matter with the fellow? It's only bird shot." 'The Honourable' strode across to the wall and looked over. I could not hear the ensuing conversation, but I saw his wallet come out. As he moved away he called out. "Get back up your pole like a good chap, don't want you fouling up the scent." Then he called across to the judge. The poor lady was really in quite a state. "The second 'cock' is lying on the verge, three or four yards beyond the telegraph pole – stone dead."

Number one made a very moderate job of the first 'cock'. It had fallen into a clump of briars. However, positively tiptoeing through these, it eventually collected it. Then it was Sally's turn. Whilst the wall, on our side, was only about four feet in one place, there was a drop of a good six to seven feel to the road. Nothing daunted, Sally was over and gone from sight. Suddenly the linesman called out from his vantage point.

"She has the bird, so she has, isn't she the great one. I'm telling you though she'll no get back." There was silence for a moment and then the commentary continued. "She's away down the road as though ole Nick himself were after her. My, but isn't she the one, away up the tree, climbin' like a cat so she is." This left us all flummoxed as to what was happening. Having consulted my judge, I went forward to the wall to see. About thirty yards down the road there was a tree that had been growing outside the demesne, but had been blown over and was now leaning against the wall. Sally had made her way up this and I was just in time to see her reach the top of the wall before jumping back into the wood.

We continued for several hundred yards. There was shooting away to our left, but apparently nothing down as the line only stopped momentarily. A cock pheasant rose out of the rough and number two gun dropped it into a large patch of laurel – it was obviously a strong runner. Number one was again sent, but much to the owners annoyance and surprise, would not go into cover. It was called up and Sally was sent. She had seen the pheasant down, as indeed had the first dog, and went crashing into the laurels, only to emerge seconds later, hackles bristling.

Her owner looked puzzled, called Sally back and asked permission of the judge to go forward to see if he could discover what it was that had deterred both dogs. The judge readily agreed, although strictly speaking, she was the one who should have done this. Willie disappeared into the laurels, to reappear seconds later. "There's a wounded fox in there. Someone lend me a gun." Having dispatched the unfortunate creature, he returned to Sally, calmly awaiting instructions. The judge turned to me.

"Oh dear, what should I do? Oh, I suppose you'd better try again number one." However, the latter did not want to know and its unfortunate handler could not get his dog anywhere near the laurels.

Sally was sent again, disappearing at speed, to return equally quickly, moments later, bearing the fox and making a perfect retrieve to hand. This totally finished the judge. She really was very 'Mrs Featherish.'

"Ah yes, very good, but poor, poor dog. You'd better take her somewhere to clear her nose." She turned to me again. "What ought I to do?"

Before I could answer Willie MacDougald cut in. "If I was out shooting I'd expect her to get the pheasant."

"Quite so, quite so. Well….. er….. Yes, I suppose you better send your dog, the poor thing! If she can't smell anything I shan't hold it against her." Sally was gone several minutes, then she returned with a cock pheasant, it had a broken wing.

"That's the sort of dog for me" said 'The Honourable' waving the barrels of his gun in our general direction. "Damned good dog – what?" I'd had enough. As I have said I don't take kindly to looking down the wrong end of the barrels at any time, and knowing the gun was loaded, I made my feeling known in no uncertain terms. 'The Honourable' looked quite surprised and stalked away.

As he did so he gave me a look of complete disdain and remarked, "Extraordinary fellow, never heard the like."

Sally only had to 'keep her nose clean' to win the stake. This she did with ease, plus wiping the eye of three dogs on the last bird of the day – a strong runner. I've often wondered what sort of a job she'd have made of the linesman!

CHAPTER 9

'Tis frizz with the cold you'll be!'

It seemed like only yesterday that Cynthia had gone to England and returned with Rona, part of my wedding present to her. But here I was, well into another shooting season, with a daughter of Rona's, Jill, by old Dave, at my heel. Jill had all her sire's drive, love of water and a superb nose. She had added greatly to the pleasure of my shooting since I first took her out towards the end of the previous season. I now shot at Ballygar regularly, having been invited to join the syndicate.

Since doing this, we had discovered a wealth of snipe shooting around Athlone. This had been achieved with the aid of a keen local wildfowler. Personally he was disinterested in snipe, but had worked up a good day's shooting for us in the area. This, together with Ballygar, Banagher, Portumna – seventeen miles down the river, where the Shannon ran into Lough Derg and literally dozens and dozens of marshes through Meath and Westmeath, meant, had we been able to spare the time, we could have shot every day of the week. However, whilst we were all very busy, most weeks we managed one or two days and, very occasionally, three. Unfortunately, quite often, I had to drop out at the last minute, usually to cope with some ducal whim. Frequently, that was all it would be – a whim!

It was late in November. There had been tremendous flooding throughout the west of the country. The water had started to recede, when a message was received from Ballygar. The whole area was 'crawling with snipe'. There hadn't been as many seen around for years. George McVeagh phoned me on a Wednesday evening, just as I arrived home, having been down to the Bruree Stud. Everything, he told me, was organised for us to leave for Athlone on Friday evening and shoot at Ballygar the next day. I prayed there would be no sudden message for me to go to England.

Fortunately my prayers were answered. I went down to Athlone under my own steam. George, together with Jim, Willie and Bobby Ganly came straight from Dublin. I was getting over a very heavy cold and, much to the amusement of my companions, I announced I was going to wear waders. Bobby said it was money-on that I would fill them up within the first hour and that I would be much better getting wet as usual. After dinner, the inevitable planning for the next day, entirely dominated by Jim and George, occupied the remainder of the evening until we all headed for bed.

We were out at the shoot before there was sufficient light to make a start. I was dropped off, with Jill, at Ballyforan Bridge, the most easterly point of the shoot. Bobby took my vehicle on and it was arranged that he would leave the case containing my dry clothes at Jim's cottage and then take the car to the Iron Bridge for me to collect at the end of my walk. The bridge was a good three to four miles up the River Suck from where I was to start. As I stood on the road, waiting for enough light, the wind grew steadily stronger, whipping up a few white horses on the river.

The forecast had been gale force winds. I was getting colder and, although there was barely enough light, I decided to get going. The river was running just below bank level, well above normal. Fifty yards from the road I had to cross a big drain. Difficult enough when the river was low, impossible, I was to find, when at its current height. There was only one thing for it, continue up the drain away from the river until I found a place where I could get over. I hadn't gone far before I put the first snipe in my bag, then another. At least it wasn't a wasted walk, even if it was not what I had planned.

The ditch curled round towards the road. Some fifty or sixty yards from this, I came to an old tree stump jutting out into the drain, reducing the distance to be cleared by nearly half. I tested the stump and it seemed strong enough. I stood on it, threw my game bag over, then my coat, pockets stuffed with cartridges and, finally, with great care, my gun. I wished I hadn't been wearing waders, it would have been an easy distance to clear in normal gear. I jumped into the air in an attempt to build up some impetus and, as I landed on 'my spring board', there was a sickening crack. The next second water was over my head. Spluttering, I started to scramble out. I was just getting a foothold when, bang, something struck me on the shoulders. It was Jill, trying to clear the drain in one. The impact sent me under again. I was not amused!

The bank was slippery and it took me several minutes to clamber out. I was absolutely soaked and other than my coat I hadn't a dry stitch. I stood gasping, wondering if I should go out onto the road and start walking towards Jim O'Briens, hoping for a lift, but realised the chances of getting one were remote to say the least. There was only one thing for it, strip off, wring out my clothes and go on shooting. I pulled off my waders and poured out several gallons of water, then divested myself of each article of clothing wringing the water out as I did so. I was turning blue with cold; up to that moment of time I had never really thought it possible! The wind continued to rise and the cold got colder. Having clambered into my sodden underpants, I realised that, before I put on the rest of my clothes I had to warm up the icicle that had replaced my body. I started running round in circles, leaping in the air and flapping my arms around my near numb torso. Jill thought it the greatest fun and rushed round with me, several times nearly bringing me crashing to the ground, but I was beginning to feel a slight tingle as I continued to race around in a circle like some maddened dervish.

Suddenly I heard peals of laughter and then. "Begob, isn't that a fine figure of a man an' him bathing on a day like this." I sprinted for my heap of soggy clothes. I had forgotten the road! Hastily I pulled on my trousers, before I even looked towards it. There, sitting sideways on an ass-cart, were two ladies of ample proportions, dressed in black, shawls tied around their heads, positively convulsed with laughter. Even the donkey between the shafts was looking in my direction. I continued to pull on my saturated clothing, no easy task with an icy wind blowing and near dead fingers. At last I was dressed. Teeth chattering, I headed towards the two ladies, who were still laughing fit to bust. I felt I should explain my actions. I had no idea how long they had been there.

I told them what had happened and apologised if I had caused them any embarrassment. This led to further laughter. "Embarrassment is it? Hasn't Bridie an' I seen more naked men than there are beads on the rosary. I've nine grand big sons, so I have, for starters. I'm telling' you it was a great sight you made leppin' around an' waving yer arms!" She stopped laughing. Her expression changed to one of concern. "My, but you could catch yer death so you could, 'tis frizz with th' cold you'll be. I know just the thing to warm you so I do." With that she started to pull up her ample skirt. My mind boggled. Whatever was going to happen next? The skirt continued to rise, exposing a mammoth knee, to be followed by thigh of equal proportion, encased in bright red bloomers. She put her hand inside the elastic and, with a flourish, produced a small medicine bottle of clear liquid – poteen! Never had I been so glad to see the fiery liquid. Without a word she passed me the bottle. Gratefully I took it, raised it towards her, 'sláinte' and took a swig. The raw spirit seemed to pass through my entire body in a matter of seconds. I revelled in the warmth it generated. It was bliss.

"Drink away, I has plenty. Me sister Kate has a grand still so she has, just outside the town. I fills me bottle every day an' keep it in me drawers. That way my Liam won't get his hands on it." I took another gulp. I felt as though I was on fire! I corked the bottle and handed it back to my benefactress, who returned it to its hiding place! I thanked her profusely. "'Tis nothing, only what any decent Christian soul would do." With that she took up the reins, gave the donkey a 'scalp' with a light stick that had been lying on the floor of the cart and, still laughing, headed off towards Ballygar.

As I turned away from the road, it suddenly dawned in me how stupid I had been. Had I carried on to the road, I could have crossed the drain without any trouble! I started to jog back towards the river. As I did so memories of yesteryear came to mind, of mother chiding me for taking some garment out of the airing cupboard and wearing it before she considered it properly dried! Snipe were everywhere and in spite of my wet clothes and the general discomfort, my eye was well and truly in. It was obvious that there must have been a very large number of migratory birds come in on the last full moon, which had been at the beginning of the week. I was quickly into double figures of snipe, as I followed the riverbank. I had just arrived opposite an island, in the centre of the river, when I spotted a flock of teal coming straight towards me, flying low into the wind. I dived for cover in a nearby ditch and standing up to shoot just before they reached me, dropped three onto the island.

I had just reloaded, when a flock of golden plover appeared flying almost the same line. I took a right and left of these. They too fell on the island. Now it was up to Jill. The river was in spate and there was quite a wave, caused by the, now, really strong wind blowing directly against the flow. However, she was very experienced, having swum since she was four months old. I had no qualms about her ability. I moved up river, above the island, before sending her. She did not attempt to fight the current, but went diagonally across and landed halfway down the island. She had certainly seen the teal fall and quickly disappeared into the rough grass and rushes, to equally quickly reappear carrying two. Obviously she was economising on effort!

She landed seventy to eighty yards down the bank from where I stood and came galloping back. The manoeuvre was repeated, bringing the third teal to hand. After a short breather Jill once more returned to the island. She was halfway back with one of the plover when suddenly, I was nearly knocked over by a freak gust of wind, causing sheets of spray to fly off the river, whipping up a heavy wave as it did so.

Through my now nebulous view, I was just able to discern Jill, before she disappeared under the water! I raced down to the bank and stopped opposite where I had last seen her. Frantically I peered through the swirling spray, but there wasn't a sign of her. My heart sank. I had horrific thoughts of her being drowned. Then, just as suddenly as the wind had reached such force, it subsided. The mist cleared and there, nearly a hundred yards down the river, was Jill, only yards from the bank. With a gasp of relief I ran to meet her. She appeared totally untroubled, but very ready to be the recipient of my outward show of relief. The last plover remained on the island. I wasn't going to ask Jill to go back, in case there was another fierce gust. I continued my walk, my game-bag growing ever fuller. It was beginning to positively bulge. By the time I reached my car I was wet, but warm. I drove back to Jim's cottage, changed my clothes and had a scalding cup of Jim's well-brewed tea. Then I went off to pick George up.

I found him sitting on the side of the road, just outside Ballygar. I jumped out of the car. George stood up. "You're late." He looked me up and down. "Looks as though Bobby was right. I suppose you filled your waders and had to go and change?" I agreed. I did not elaborate. I knew my friends. The leg pulling would be never ending and certainly I was not going to say anything about the lady with the poteen in her knickers. We went off to do a walk on the Ballygar Bog. We hadn't gone far, when a pack of five or six grouse rose in front of George, but out of range. One swung back towards me, climbing fast in the strong wind. I swung on it and pulled the trigger. A hit, but from the way it planed down, it was going to be a strong runner. I saw Jill watching it and sent her at once. It came down a good hundred and fifty yards from where I stood. Jill owned the fall immediately and went racing off across the bog. She must have gone the better part of a hundred yards, when suddenly she made a dive into what appeared to be an extra thick clump of heather. I saw the grouse momentarily as it fluttered up. She leapt in the air, caught it and came galloping back. Moments later she delivered it to hand. There were a smattering of grouse on all the red-bogs around Ballygar and we quite frequently saw them, but seldom got a shot at one. It was always something of an occasion when one was added to the bag.

By the time we returned to the car it was approaching lunchtime. We headed off back through the village for Jim's cottage. George insisted we should stop at Markie Wall's. Markie ran an establishment much the same as J.J.'s, but without the additional businesses round the back. However, he did have other interests such as auctioneering and dealing in wool. Years before I arrived in Ireland my friends used to stay at Markie's. However, to the annoyance of all concerned he was stopped from letting rooms because he hadn't, as Jim O'Brien put it 'a flash lavatory'. Markie was in the shop as we entered and gave us his usual friendly welcome. We went through to the bar. Without asking, Markie drew a pint of Guinness for George and enquired what I would have. I settled for a shandy.

Mine host looked at George and winked. "I hear tell they're starting a nudist colony out at Ballyforan."

"Oh, I haven't heard anything about this. Tell me more." George looked enquiringly at Markie.

"Well, it seems a man was seen running around soon after daylight, leaping in the air and near stark naked he was. Then he got all dressed up, long rubber boots and all. It seems he had a gun and a dog with him too." The story was out! The ladies had not been slow in spreading the news. I knew the incident was going to take a lot of living down. It seemed that the whole district knew. Lunch was punctuated by sly jibes and quips from my friends and it was not until we had nearly finished our meal that we got down to the serious business of deciding where we would shoot during the afternoon. A quick count revealed that it could be on to shoot one hundred and fifty snipe in the day, something that, as yet, we had not achieved.

Bobby and I went off to shoot the Horseshoe Bog, according to my companion, a seven mile trek. I was not entirely enamoured with the idea. I had not forgotten my first visit to Ballygar with George. For years it had been acclaimed as 'the home of snipe', particularly when the migratory birds arrived. In spite of its reputation it had never produced anything very spectacular since I had been a member of the shoot. Once again in failed to live up to it's former greatness. We came across pockets of snipe and, when we did, scored fairly consistently, but saw nothing like the number that Bobby had been so confident we would find. By the time we returned to the car we had added about a score to the bag.

As usual, before returning to our hotel in Athlone, we took Jim O'Brien into Markie Wall's for a 'bit of gas' with the locals. Jimmy Langan joined us, did a count and tied up the birds. 149 snipe, we had missed the magic figure by one! 14 golden plover, 3 teal, 3 mallard, 2 widgeon and 1 grouse – a total of 172 head. It was a memorable day from more aspects than one, or at least as far as I was concerned. Strangely, I did not suffer anything from my ducking and the subsequent two and a half to three hours spent in wet clothes. It confirmed what one old character once said to us at Banagher, as we walked out of his rushy fields, soaked to the skin and the rain driving across the callows. "Good day men. A soft day it is, but I'm thinking as long as you stay hot you'll never get cold."

His comment might sound a bit 'Irish', but his meaning was clear. As long as one kept moving and kept warm, all would be well. So it was on that day, although soaked, thanks to the lady and her poteen and walking hard until I could change my clothes, I did not get a chill. In the twenty years that I shot snipe I cannot remember neither I, nor any of my companions being any the worse from a good wetting.

It was early in December and there was an estate function in London, which I had to attend. Cynthia was invited. When it was over, she went off to Malvern to stay with her brother, whilst I returned to Ireland. It was the first time I had been at Bryanstown, since we were married, that she had been away. I missed her, so did the dogs. We now had five Goldens and, rain or fine, six days a week they accompanied Cynthia as she rode Drenagh out at exercise.

On the Thursday evening I was thoroughly bored. There was no shoot organised for the weekend. George, who amongst his illustrious clients numbered the Aga Khan, would not leave home. The latter was proposing to visit his Stud Farm in Co. Kildare. George had to be on stand-by over the weekend in case his presence was required. Jim had been invited to a pheasant shoot and my other Ganly friends had various commitments. I decided to phone the Corrib Hotel and have a chat with Peter. He was, I knew, 'a regular' virtually every evening from around eight thirty to ten. This one proved to be no exception and, after some preliminary chat, Peter told me that a coot shoot was being organised on Corrib for the coming Saturday. It sounded interesting and, after a brief word with Derek to make sure he'd have room for me, I said I would be there on Friday evening.

I drove the entire way from Maynooth in a howling gale and torrential rain. By the time I reached my destination I was seriously querying the wisdom of having left the comfort of my home. However, a couple of 'jars' with Peter and Derek, followed by an excellent dinner, brought things back into the right perspective. I was ready for anything. Quite a crowd had gathered in the bar, whilst I had been in the dining room. Most of them were participants, one way or another, in the shoot. I knew the majority. Much planning and drinking ensued, that was to continue into the small hours of the morning.

Around eleven thirty, the sergeant and one of the garda came across from the Barracks. The former remarked that it was time everyone went home, accepted my offer of a drink and settled himself comfortably for the remainder of the 'meeting'. Finally it was agreed that four boats, each with two guns, would anchor across 'The Narrows'. Two boats would leave at daylight to go up to the head of the lough, whilst two more would head down for Galway. These would then drive the coots over the guns. With the vast area of water involved, I was very sceptical as to whether this would work. It was then that Peter told me that it was exactly the same strategy they had brought into being several times before and with great success.

The following morning I joined Peter at his boat soon after 10.00 a.m. The wind had dropped considerably from the day before, but there was still a stiff breeze and quite a lot of wave. I climbed into the boat and as I did so, noticed something long, wrapped in a length of tarpaulin, lying in the bottom of the boat. I enquired what it was. Peter told me it was a double barrelled 8 bore that had belonged to his grandfather. He went on to say that, if I was agreeable, after the coot drive, he thought we ought to go looking for widgeon. Apparently he had seen some huge flocks about recently and no one had been after them.

Three quarters of an hour later the four boats were anchored across 'The Narrows'. It had been a fairly wet and bumpy journey. The lough was still decidedly choppy and the lowering sky did not promise any improvement in the weather, but at least it was dry overhead. The wind, I noted, as we sat patiently awaiting the thousands of coot predicted in the snug warmth of the bar around 2.00 a.m., was blowing straight down the lough towards Galway. I felt our quarry would have to be very hard pushed to fly into such a wind. After about an hour, with the boat bouncing on the waves, whilst it became increasingly cold, I at last spotted the two boats coming from the direction of Galway. There was no sign of the vast quantity of coots that should have been preceding them!

Soon, however, it was possible to see small numbers getting up and immediately turning back with the wind. It seemed that no way were they going to come forward. I looked up the lough, just in time to see a solitary coot approaching. It went high over the right hand boat. A shot rang out, and, to my surprise it crumpled and fell. Ten minutes passed and not as much as a seagull came near. Suddenly Peter said 'look' as he pointed up the lough. The sky was almost black with widgeon, hundreds and hundreds of them. They were well out of range when they came straight over the boats moored across 'The Narrows'. Fortunately no one wasted any cartridges! Peter watched them intently and then smiled. "I know where we'll find them. There's a sheltered bay four to five miles down the lough. We'll pay it a visit when the drive's over."

Just as he said this a number of coots started to appear. I was surprised at the height and speed at which they flew; although the latter wasn't really surprising in view of the following wind. They made very sporting targets and certainly were not easy to hit sitting in a boat, bobbling about and every few seconds coming up short on the anchor rope! After about twenty minutes 'the beaters' joined us. Not one coot had come over the guns from the direction of Galway. Anchors were pulled in and we started to pick-up. This was done by slowly cruising round and round, scooping out the coots with the landing nets. This took nearly half an hour before Peter was satisfied that we had left none.

Then all eight boats made for a nearby island and ran in on a sandy beach on the lee side. Derek produced a bottle of 'the hard stuff' and a crate of Guinness. Whilst the party were refreshing themselves, Peter collected the birds from the various boats and counted the bag – 81 coots and 1 shoveler. He was very disappointed and said that the last time they had shot more than four times as many. I remarked that it really didn't matter, we'd all had plenty of shooting and they didn't do any harm anyway. I was quickly corrected over this by several of the gillies. They assured me that they caused devastation to trout fry and more would have been welcome as they were excellent eating. I didn't argue, but felt the coots in Ireland were probably much the same as those in England and lived largely off submerged plants. However, there can always be exceptions to every rule and I did not pursue the matter further.

When everyone was refreshed, seven of the boats set out for Oughterard, taking the morning's bag with them. Peter told them we were going off to look for duck around the islands. As soon as we were alone Peter unwrapped his 8 bore. It was a magnificent old hammer gun with damascus barrels and in really excellent condition. The cartridge cases were brass. The original owner loaded his own with, of course, black powder. Peter had had this done by a gunsmith friend in Galway. We set off down the lough, the wind freshening all the time. Peter made full use of the islands to get all the shelter he could, for there was quite a wave running in some of the more open parts. In fact several times, much to Peter's amusement, I thought we were going to be pooped as we surged forward on an extra big wave.

After about half an hour we approached a point of the mainland that ran well out into the lough. As we rounded this Peter cut the engine and, at the same time, told me to get down into the bottom of the boat. Fortunately I had oilskin trousers on, for we had shipped quite a lot of water. My companion too crouched down below the gunwale. We drifted into the bay. After ten to fifteen minutes Peter cautiously peered over the edge of the boat. "I was right, they're here." With equal stealth I too took a look. There, some three to four hundred yards away was the biggest flock of widgeon I had ever seen and I'd seen some very big ones on the Shannon! There must have been in the region of a thousand.

As I looked quickly around, it seemed as though the wind would, eventually, blow us straight to them. It was far calmer in the bay.

Peter crawled up the boat nearer to me and, almost lying in the bottom with water gently swilling around us, we made our plans. Peter kindly offered me the opportunity to use his big gun, but I knew he was longing to try it out and insisted that he should fire it. Slowly we drifted towards our quarry. It seemed like eternity, but at last we could hear them quite plainly. The adrenaline flowed. The boat seemed to be almost becalmed in the now near smooth water. Twice I heard some of the huge flock take off, only to land seconds later, but still we remained cramped in the bottom of the boat. At last Peter said 'now' and stood up. The whole sky seemed to be filled with widgeon. As the ancient gun boomed twice, black smoke partly obliterated my view, but not sufficiently to stop me seeing a cloud of duck coming straight for us. I stood up and took a most pleasing right and left, reloaded and downed a third. We shot several wounded birds on the water, which had been diving as we approached them, before deciding we had picked everything, making a total of nineteen.

Peter turned the boat and headed out of the bay for an island where, he said, there was a sheltered beach that we could land on, pull the boat up, light a fire to boil a kettle and have lunch. I looked at my watch. It was already 2.30 p.m.. No wonder I was feeling hungry! When we had the fire going, I produced a lemonade bottle into which I had asked Derek to put two large Powers before I had left the hotel that morning. I poured us each a dram; it certainly went down well, for it was becoming increasingly cold. When we'd finished lunch, Peter suggested we should take a walk around the island to loosen up a bit. He claimed he was stiff from crouching down for so long in the bottom of the boat.

As we topped the bank leading up from the beach I immediately noticed smoke rising from amongst some big boulders at the far end of the island. I asked if it was inhabited. The reply was in the negative and, smiling, Peter headed for the smoke. Within minutes we came across what, for me, was an odd scene. There were a number of small barrels, a coil made out of copper piping and a 'brew' bubbling away over the turf fire, but no sign of anyone. Peter called out in Gaelic. Three men appeared almost immediately from behind nearby rocks. We had landed by some extraordinary chance, or was it, on an island where three Galway lads, Peter told me, were preparing poteen for the Christmas market. Considerable chat ensued, in which I took no part, for it was all in Irish. Eventually Peter asked me if I had £2 on me. I had. These plus three brace of widgeon, procured us two one gallon stone jars of the illicit throat skinning alcohol. After some more chat, this time in English, Peter said it was time we were on our way.

When we were clear of the island, it became apparent that the wind was freshening all the time. We had a rough journey back, most of which I spent sitting on the bottom of the boat in the bow acting as ballast! It was as well that I had a good oilskin coat, trousers and a sou'wester, otherwise I would have been soaked. Apart from acting as ballast I had to cradle the two jars, to make sure they did not break! By the time we reached the river I felt as though I must be black and blue from all the bangs I received as the boat cracked down on the waves. I stiffly clambered up off the bottom of the boat and sat astride the forward thwart. It was getting dark.

As we turned a bend in the river I heard Peter draw in his breath. He threw me a sack and barely whispering said. "Put the jars into the bag and start filling it with widgeon – quick." Without looking round I did as I was told, wondering at the haste. Just when the boat bumped again the bank I heard a voice behind me. "Good night Peter, good night sorr. 'Tis well you're safe. With this wind we were getting worried, so we were."

I looked round, it was the sergeant. My heart missed a beat; even in those days there were heavy fines for being in possession of poteen. The sergeant helped Peter moor and unload the boat and, being the 'dacent' man he was, carried the sack up to my car!

CHAPTER 10

'Paddy and the Prince'

It was very difficult in the early fifties to find the time to even fractionally take advantage of all the wonderful sporting opportunities that were available throughout the year. When the shooting ended and the hunting season was coming to a close, so the trout and salmon fishing started. Although, to be strictly accurate, the latter started on the River Liffey on the 1st of January, well before the end of the shooting season. Every year stout-hearted men and, occasionally some equally brave women, would line the river banks on New Year's day above Island Bridge; all intent on claiming the publicity that went with catching the first salmon of the season. This was usually sold for some quite outrageous price to one of the leading Dublin hotels – a prestige purchase! My heart was never stout enough, nor my enthusiasm so great that it led me to participate in the annual gathering. One enthusiast told me that he had fished the Liffey on the 1st January for 29 years. He had never caught a fish! Apparently one found a place on the crowded bank as dawn broke and there you remained all day, casting across the same bit of water until dark or one's fanatical ardour waned.

No, the Liffey wasn't for me. My favourite spot was Ballynahinch, in the heart of Connemara. At one time a private fishery but, eventually, the house was turned into a hotel which could boast some seven miles of private salmon river and a number of loughs, the best of which was Lough Inagh, my favourite. At one stage in its history, Ballynahinch was owned by the famous cricketing Indian Prince – Ranjitsinhji. What drew him to that part of the world I never discovered, for rumour has it that His Highness was certainly no fisherman when he purchased the property, but it appeared he was keen to learn. Towards this end he instructed one of his gillies, Paddy, I forget his surname, but it would be a fair bet, in that part of the country, that it would be Joyce, to initiate him into the art of fly-fishing.

Over the years I am sure that the ensuing story lost nothing in the telling but Paddy remained very consistent in his version and 'dined out' on it or, to be more accurate, 'wined out' on it for many years. Paddy was an old man when I first met him, virtually retired, largely due to being almost crippled with rheumatism. What ever else the latter may have affected, it certainly had had no ill effects on his swallow! It normally took two, sometimes three pints of porter for the tale of 'Paddy and the Prince' to unfold.

Paddy, for a number of days, took his employer into a grass field and made him practice casting with a massive two handed salmon rod. History relates that the Prince was a quick learner and so, Paddy decided, the time had come to try the real thing. Accompanied by another gillie, Paddy took the Prince to a famous beat on the river, Green Point. Conditions were perfect. There had been a spate, which had let up a fresh run of fish and the river had dropped back to be at an ideal level. Paddy put up the rod and, after consultation with his colleague, selected a fly and set the Prince to work. In spite of the barbed hook passing dangerously close to Paddy's ear, he remained by his pupil, giving advice and encouragement. Soon the Prince was getting the line out well and, after about twenty minutes Paddy saw the line tighten.

"Begob, yer have one, Highness. Strike man, strike!" The Prince did what he was told, driving the hook home. The line screamed off the reel as the salmon powered up the river. "That's right Highness, keep a steady pressure on him. My, but he's big so he is. I'm telling you that's a twenty pounder or more." By this time, according to his colleague, Paddy was jumping around with excitement. The salmon made several more wild runs, each time the Prince exerted just the right amount of pressure, it seemed as though the fish was beginning to tire.

"You has him bate. Gently now sorr an' he's ours." Paddy picked up his long handled gaff and advanced towards the riverbank. As he did so the salmon leapt high in the air. Paddy almost screamed at the Prince. "Drop the point of the rod."

Too late. Instinctively the Prince whipped back the rod, the line tightened as the salmon was still out of the water, the hook was out, it was gone. Paddy hurled his cap to the ground and jumped on it. "Jasus, yer great black stupid bastard." Paddy was nearly crying with frustration. With most employers, such an outburst would have warranted immediate dismissal. Ranjitsinhji, however, walked over to Paddy, put his hand on the gillie's shoulder.

"Black – yes, stupid – yes, bastard – no. Come on Paddy, we'll catch another and this time I'll do better." It was not long before the Prince hooked another fish. He made no mistakes this time and soon a fine twelve pounder was on the bank. Now, if one was getting the three pint version, and one usually did, this was about the time that Paddy began to wonder if he had gone too far when reproaching his employer. The Prince decided he had had enough, handed the rod over to the other gillie to go on fishing and told Paddy to accompany him to the house. Here Paddy was told to go through to the study and wait.

This, he said, made him certain that he was 'for the chop'. He began to deeply regret his outburst for there were virtually no other jobs around other than on the Prince's property. A few minutes later his employer returned, followed by the butler bearing a silver salver, on which was a decanter of whisky and two tumblers. When the butler had departed, the Prince poured out two half tumblers of whisky and passed one to his gillie. He raised his glass towards Paddy. "Well here's to my first salmon and may there be many more to come. From now on Paddy I only want you to gillie for me."

Having said this, they finished their drinks in silence and the Prince sent Paddy on his way, but not before he had pressed a fiver into Paddy's hand—a small fortune in the West of Ireland in those days. Paddy always finished his story with "Stupid black bastard he was when he lost that salmon but I'm telling you, there was no greater gentleman nor there was."

All that had been many years before I first went to Ballynahinch. I enjoyed fishing Inagh more than the river. I loved the wild grandeur of the surrounding mountains, with the Twelve Pins towering in the background, the isolation and lack of human depredation. But, apart from the surroundings, I found the fishing more exciting, for as well as salmon there was always a prodigious run of white trout (sea trout) in the late summer and autumn. Further, unlike many of the loughs and rivers the season did not close at the end of September, but continued on into the first two weeks of October.

So it was that, towards the end of September, I found I had nine days clear of meetings and other engagements and, on the spur of the moment, telephoned Ballynahinch Hotel to see if they had a room for Cynthia and me. They had. Cynthia had become very keen on fishing, but had never been to Inagh. When Jim Ganly heard what we were planning, he arranged that he and his wife, Doodie, would join us for the latter part of our stay. We took our time driving across, stopping at Oughterard on the way to see our many friends and acquaintances, arriving at our destination in time for dinner. Looking back the charges seem quite ridiculous. The hotel cost £26 per week all in. This included free fishing on Inagh, but a charge of £2 per day was made for fishing the river, one of the best in the British Isles. One paid the gillies direct. John Joyce, the head gillie on Inagh, who I normally went out with charged £1 per day for his boat and services and a further £1 a day for the use of his outboard motor, if one had not got one's own. This did not include the petrol!

On the first morning of our holiday we arrived out at Lough Inagh around 10.00 a.m. John was waiting for us. Conditions, he assured us, were ideal. There was a light westerly wind, just enough to produce a gentle wave. The sun shone, highlighting the heather that spread as far as the eye could see. It was beautiful, but still retained the rugged harshness that made one realise that both man and beast had to work for survival in this inexorable countryside. As I put up the rods, two spinning and two fly rods, a salmon jumped, not twenty yards from where we stood. John told us that there had been an exceptional run of both salmon and trout, but surprisingly few had been caught. This he put down to two things. Firstly, there had been a series of inexperienced anglers fishing the lough over the past few weeks, but more than this he blamed the fact that for days and days there had been a cold easterly wind. I was reminded of the old jingle my grandfather, a brilliant fly fisherman, had taught me when I was about seven.

When the wind is in the north,
Then the fishes don't come forth.
When the wind is in the south,
They take the bait with open mouth.
When the wind is in the east,
Then the fishes bite the least.
When the wind is in the west,
Then the fishes bite the best.

Over the years I found this to be remarkably true. According to John, the wind had only backed round to the west twenty-four hours before our arrival.

John suggested that we should troll up to the top of the lough and then do a drift back, close to the shore. As soon as we were clear of the landing, I picked up one of the spinning rods, cast well out to the side, letting out plenty of line as the bait, a Hardy's Yellow Belly, came round behind the slow moving boat, before handing it to Cynthia. I did the same with the second rod, resting it against a thole pin and tucking the butt under my knee as I filled my pipe.

I had only just got the latter going to my satisfaction and was happily watching three ravens, as they soared several thousand feet above us, when the tranquillity was broken by a positive whoop from Cynthia. "Reel your line in, I've got one!"

Hastily I did as I was bid, as the line screamed off Cynthia's reel. John turned the boat in the direction the salmon was taking out towards the islands. The rod bent double, as the line cut through the water. Suddenly, like a giant silver bullet, the salmon leapt high into the air. Like old Paddy and the Price, I shouted at Cynthia to drop the point of her rod, but she was ahead of me. As the fish disappeared back into the water, the line went slack. "Oh, it's gone."

"No it hasn't. It's coming back this way. Reel in, but be careful when the line tightens again. Don't put too much pressure on." Seconds later Cynthia was again in contact with her quarry. As soon as the fish felt the line become taught, it again launched itself into the air, quite close to the boat. I got a better look at it. It was a good fish by Inagh standards, where a twenty pounder was a whopper. Ten minutes and three jumps later, John lent over the side of the boat and deftly gaffed the first fish of our holiday. I suddenly realised too, it was Cynthia's first salmon! I took a spring balance out of my bag and weighed it – a seventeen and a half pound cock fish. Cynthia's face was alight with pleasure as she surveyed her catch. Turning to me she said, "We'll have that one smoked."

There was no problem in those days getting fish up to Dublin, even from the wilds of Connemara. All one had to do was write the labels. The hotel would pack the fish, put them on the early bus from Clifden to Galway, which passed the entrance to the hotel grounds and the bus dropped them off at the station.

We trolled on up to the top of the lough without further excitements, although we saw a number of salmon jumping. This didn't please me greatly, for on previous visits I had noticed that when this happened, one seldom caught one, but when all went quiet – watch out! The best day I ever had on Inagh, seven salmon averaging eleven and a half pounds, I never saw one jump all day. We started our drift, after I had moved Cynthia so that when she brought her line back to cast, it came back over the water. She wasn't that expert as yet with a fly rod. I didn't want a hook in my ear or the back of my neck! The second cast I made produced a lovely head and tail rise to my dropper. I struck at the right moment. The result was a two and a half pound white trout, fresh from the sea, that fought magnificently. John smiled, he was a man of few words; he looked up at the sky before saying. "'Tis a grand day an' I'm thinking you'll have the boat filled by night."

We didn't quite do that, but by the time we went in to the top island for lunch where there was a hut, we had Cynthia's salmon, plus a lovely fresh run hen fish, still with sea lice on it, which I took on the fly and five sea trout all over two pounds. We had put back at least a dozen trout of 1lb or less. Whilst John got a fire going to boil the kettle, Cynthia unpacked our lunch and I poured a couple of gin and tonics for us and a Guinness for John. We sat down in the shade. The sun was really hot. John raised his glass. "Sláinte. I hear Mr. Ganly and his lady are coming in about a week. I'm thinking he'll be trying to get her out to fish again, but terrible obstinate she is." Doodie was no fisherwoman. She claimed one lunatic in the family was enough.

The afternoon proved as exciting as the morning. Cynthia caught another salmon as we trolled up to the top of the lough immediately after lunch, to start another drift. A twin to the one I had killed before lunch. The trout remained hyperactive. I caught a three and a half pounder, the best I ever took from Inagh. By the time we returned to the landing we had three salmon and fourteen white trout all over 2lbs. They made a fine sight, laid out on the marble slab in the billiard room back at the hotel where catches were normally displayed.

On our way back we called at Nora Milne's – the Queen of Connemara – for a drink. A visit to Nora's was a must if fishing Inagh. In fact it almost took the form of a ritual! The pub was a corrugated iron sheeting hut attached to her small thatched cottage. Except that drink was not being sold illegally, it could well have passed for a shebeen. Seating was limited to a couple of planks resting on empty beer cases and one wooden stool at the bar. The choice of drinks was nearly as limited as the seating, but the main essentials were always available

– porter, whiskey and gin.

Nora's husband had been head gillie on Inagh. He had been drowned when caught out in a sudden storm, many years before I knew her. She was a tremendous character. Her daughter, whose name, alas, I have long since forgotten, but always thought of as 'Annie Oakley' was perhaps an even greater one. She was a strikingly attractive girl, tall, slim and usually dressed like a man, which in those days was very unusual in the West of Ireland. She had an ebullient personality with a great sense of humour. Meet her outside her home and, more often than not, she had a .22 rifle slung over her shoulder. She was a quite remarkable shot.

One evening, when Jim and I had called in after fishing, I was ribbing her about her shooting. She became somewhat irritated and bet me £5 that she could shoot a half crown from between my finger and thumb, at twenty paces. I declined, but she insisted that we go outside to prove her marksmanship. Three times she stuck a penny in a tee of mud on top of a post. Three times she strode away from it, turned at about twenty paces and fired, almost as she did so. Three times the penny went spinning away into the heather!

Perfect day followed perfect day, both from the point of view of weather and sport. Never had I experienced fishing like it and, for that matter, never have since those memorable days. By the time Jim and Doodie arrived, Cynthia and I were burned nearly black from wind and sun. There were three fishing days left before we had to depart. Jim, much to Doodie's satisfaction, decided to fish the river. This meant that she could stroll down to his allotted beat, make suitable noises as she put it and return to the comfort of the hotel.

After breakfast, Cynthia and I again set forth for Inagh, whilst Jim headed for the river. Not all the beats had been booked so, as a regular, he had been told he could fish three. He tried to persuade Cynthia and me to join him on the river, saying that the latter always fished better than Inagh. However, we stuck to our guns and headed off for the lough. When we arrived the surface was like a sheet of glass, not a ripple on it. John was very pessimistic. He claimed that the prospects of any wind were virtually nil and catching any trout even worse. Did we want to go out and troll for salmon? He obviously thought we should, so did Cynthia. I had little choice other than to agree, but said I would spin. Cynthia looked at me pityingly and said she saw no point in unnecessary work!

John moved the boat out from the shore. Cynthia let her line out, propped the rod up against a thole pin and, with a sigh of contentment, made herself comfortable and prepared to relax in the hot sunshine. I started to spin, having first lit my pipe. There wasn't enough wind to blow the smoke away from my face! I cast all around the boat and kept on doing so for half an hour. I changed the lure and the result was the same. After another half hour, I changed the bait again, but to no avail. There wasn't a ripple on the water, not even a ring from a trout rising. I asked John if he thought it was worth staying out. He gave me a slow smile. "You never can tell with salmon. Them's terribble quare cratures so they are. Anyways, what else have you to do?"

He had a point, I kept on casting. I asked Cynthia if she would like me to change the spinner on her line. She replied that she was perfectly happy with what was on it. Hadn't we caught all our salmon on 'Yellow Bellies' so why change? After two hours I gave up. Changed the lure yet again, this time to a 'Yellow Belly', let the line out and joined Cynthia trolling. It was hot. In fact it was very hot. I reached into the picnic basked, took out a bottle of Guinness, removed the top and passed it to John. I shared a lager with Cynthia. We finished our drinks and continued on our sleepy way across the sandy bay at the top of the lough.

Suddenly I saw the tip of Cynthia's rod twitch. So did she and, picking it up, let the point back towards the stern before she struck. At that moment John drew my attention to my rod, it was bending dramatically. I picked it up, thinking that Cynthia's fish had crossed my line, but I was wrong. Her line was cutting through the water to the right of the boat, whilst mine was going with equal force in the opposite direction. For at least five minutes we kept the two salmon apart, then the inevitable happened, the lines crossed and within seconds they were both gone. John shook his head. "I've never seen that before an', with the class of a clout the missus gave hers, I'd of thought the head would have come off before the hook would of pulled out."

Cynthia was not a happy lady. For some reason, which only her particular brand of logic could explain, she blamed me for the loss of her fish. We were only a few hundred yards from the top island, Deer Island, where there was a hut, so I suggested, as it was nearly one o'clock, that we should go in for lunch. John glanced over his shoulder, obviously decided it wasn't worth starting up the outboard and began to row hard. Cynthia let her line out again. I told her that it was a waste of time and that we were moving much too fast. She gave me a disdainful look and let out more line!

There was a tremendous jerk on the point of the rod, which nearly shot over the side of the boat. Cynthia only just caught it. As she did so a salmon jumped high out of the water, a good thirty to forty yards behind the boat. John backwatered hard to stop the momentum and brought the boat around. He rowed quickly after the line that was literally zinging through the water. The line continued to fly off the reel for another few seconds, then I saw that Cynthia was getting some back. The salmon jumped again and then headed towards the boat. Cynthia's face was alight with both satisfaction and concentration. I had not said a word. Soon she was in control, then and only then did she turn to me. "See! You'll never catch fish if you don't have a bait in the water."

Several minutes later a hen fish, fresh run with sea lice still on it, lay in the bottom of the boat. I weighed it at exactly ten and a quarter pounds. Although we had one and lost two, we hadn't seen a salmon move the entire morning. We did not hurry over lunch and sat smoking and chatting after we had finished. When we eventually decided to move, it was still flat calm. Cynthia let her line out as soon as we were clear of the island. I started to spin. I found the inactivity of trolling tedious. About the fourth cast, and bang, I was into a fish. It fought like a demon and, in spite of exerting all the pressure I dared, it was nearly fifteen minutes before it lay in the bottom of the boat, a replica of Cynthia's. The afternoon passed quickly. We each had a couple of 'touches' and each killed another fish. All four were identical – ten and a quarter pounds.

It was a fantastic evening and we went ashore on the sandy beach at the head of the lough. John boiled a kettle and we enjoyed a cup of tea. Just as we were finishing I noticed a slight ripple on the water – wind! By the time we were back in the boat there was a wave, be it ever so small. Five minutes later there was enough to make me pick up a fly rod. Cynthia said she'd had enough and would watch. I told John we'd do a drift back to the landing and then call it a day. For some reason, I know not what, I had discarded my usual 11ft universal fly rod and had put up a 9ft trout rod that had belonged to my father.

I smiled to myself, as I thought what might happen if I hooked a salmon, but that was unlikely, for I had put on small flies, which almost said 'for trout only'. I worked hard, but never moved a thing. Cynthia yawned and murmured that a 'G & T' would go down well. We were nearly at the landing and, as I shot the line out, remarked that it was the last cast of the day. I started to reel the line in, as opposed to working it back by hand. It was nearly in, when suddenly it was being ripped off again. The rod was bent double, the point nearly in the water, in spite of my efforts to try and keep it up. I realised that I had little line left and was rapidly coming to the end of the backing.

I shouted to John to row harder after the fish, which was certainly no trout. Some forty yards from the boat a salmon rocketed into the air. Glancing down at my reel, I realised that John had not gained on the fish; I had only a few feet of line left. Desperately I ripped off the remainder from the reel, causing the tension to ease. The point of the rod came up, the salmon had checked its run! John continued to row hard, as I reeled in. I had regained something over half the line when I again made contact. This was the signal for another mad dash. I cursed myself for changing rods. Alas, the rod I had chosen to use was not man enough for the job I was asking it to do. We had to follow the salmon wherever it decided to go and that seemed to be a tour of the lower end of the lough!

After half an hour, applying the maximum tension that was possible I felt that at last I was beginning to get the upper hand. The wild runs were shorter and not so sustained. The light was beginning to go and Cynthia, now that the sun had disappeared behind the mountains, was becoming cold and suggested I should hurry up 'or let the wretched thing go'. Just after this the fish headed back under the boat and the line went slack. She perked up and said she thought I had lost it. Fortunately she was wrong. After about fifty minutes it went to the bottom of the lough and sulked. I tried to 'pump' it up, but again the rod just wasn't strong enough. What line I managed to gain was a painfully slow process. Things were becoming desperate. After consultation with John, I brought the line round to him. Slowly he pulled it in by hand, as I wound it onto the reel. At last I could just make out the shape of the fish. John released the line, as I exerted all the pressure I could. I saw him reach out with the gaff. The battle was over; it had taken 1 hour and 10 minutes. I looked at my capture, a cock fish, which had obviously been up in the lough for quite a while. It was a golden black colour, with a great hook on the bottom jaw. It weight 16 lbs and my rod was never the same again!

We didn't call at Nora's that evening. It was quite dark by the time we were back at the hotel. As we parked, Liam, the hall porter, came out and greeted us. "We were getting worried about you sorr. Did you have any luck?"

I told him that there were five salmon in the boot of the car. "How did they do on the river?"

"Not good, not good. Mr. Ganly has one small one so he has. They're all in the billiard room admiring it. No one else had a touch. Shall I bring yours through?" The temptation was too great. Normally, Jim caught far more than me. He was, to start with, very knowledgeable and definitely a better fisherman; in fact few were his superior. "Give me five minutes and then bring them in,"

Cynthia and I went through to where all the fishing enthusiasts congregated – the bar. Jim greeted us. Cynthia smiled, "It was a gorgeous day, fantastic sun and not a ripple all day. I've got a lovely tan." Jim also smiled and, indicating the lone fish on the slab said, "I told you, you should have come on the river. Inagh's never any good without wind."

Cynthia walked over and looked at Jim's fish. "Not very big, is it?" As she said this Liam arrived, aided by a small boy and laid out our catch on the slab.

There was silence for a few seconds and then excited queries from the English visitors. What did you catch them on? Did they fight hard? What do they weigh? Of course such queries, to any fisherman worth his salt, meant a blow by blow account of the day's happenings, particularly with regard to the last addition to our bag. Only the arrival of the manageress, enquiring as to whether any of us wanted dinner, brought the saga to an end. When we were enjoying our coffee and liqueurs, I suggested to Jim that he join us on Inagh the next day and, if it was still sunny, Doodie should come too. Neither was enthusiastic and they said they'd think about it.

The evening was spent, as was normal at Ballynahinch, sitting in the bar talking fishing. It was, indeed, one big happy family. Four of the English visitors were departing in the morning. They had been at the hotel for a week and we had become very friendly. During the early part of their stay they had been very successful on the river and had been anxious to get a fish or two on their last day to take home, but the gods had not favoured them. One eventually asked me if I would consider selling them two of ours? The answer was no. I had never sold and haven't to this day, fish, snipe, or wildfowl. Don't ask me why, for I'm not sure that I know the reason. I think, probably, because I gained so much pleasure from my fishing and shooting, that I would have had a sense of guilt in receiving monetary gain from it. I did, however, after consultation with Cynthia, say they could have the four hen fish as a present. I had already arranged to send the other one off for smoking. We had, over the last week, virtually saturated our Dublin friends with salmon and sea trout.

Rather dejectedly our English friends said that, whilst they were most appreciative, they could not possibly accept such a gift. In due course one of them went through to the hotel office; he said to make sure their bills would be ready early in the morning. Just before we were heading for bed, I was asked if the offer of the salmon still stood. I replied that it did and, with almost embarrassing thanks, it was accepted. I did not give the matter another thought, at least not until I was settling our account, just before leaving. There was a credit for 41lbs of salmon. Our friends had connived with the management!

The next day was hot again and, for the majority of the day, a replica of the previous one. However, fortune was not quite so kind, but Cynthia caught another fresh run salmon. About 3.00 p.m. a steady breeze got up and we had great sport with the white trout before calling it a day around 5.00 p.m. Our total for the nine days had risen to 22 salmon and 51 white trout, the latter averaging a little over 2lbs. Well pleased, we called at Nora's and after 'a bit of gas' with the locals, returned to the hotel.

There, almost an air of gloom pervaded. Not one fish had been taken on the river. Jim had been fishing the famous Green Point and even he was unable to tempt one to take any of the lures that he put over the multitude of fish that were known to be there. The weather forecast was the same for the morrow as it had been all the week. Jim, having seen our catch, decided he would come to Inagh the next day and went off to arrange about a boat. He soon returned to say all was fixed; he would be going out with John's cousin – John Martin Joyce. Throughout the evening we all three bullied Doodie to come too. Eventually, saying she knew she would regret it, she capitulated. Jim was delighted.

The following morning the two John's were waiting for us at the landing. The sun shone, as bright as ever, but a slight wind ruffled the surface of the lough. Conditions looked as though they could well become perfect. Doodie, still muttering, climbed into the boat. She and Jim were away first and as soon as they were clear of the land I saw Jim hand her a rod. She called out to us. "I'm mad. I know I'll regret this."

We laughed and waving, wished her luck. We were soon under way. The plan was to troll, as quickly as was feasible, to the top of the lough and then do a drift. We never moved a fish, but saw a number of salmon jumping. Our luck was no better as we kept casting our flies. The wind was increasing markedly, until Cynthia laid down her rod, saying she was going to have a rest and that she just hadn't the experience to control her line under the prevailing conditions. I continued, but we never saw a sign of a trout. There might as well not have been a fish in the lough. In fact Cynthia suggested that we had emptied it during the previous week! We were heading once more back into the wind to start another drift, passing quite close to our friends when just as we were level, Doodie let out a yell. She'd hooked a salmon. I asked John to hold hard, so that we could watch this epic event. After about ten minutes, I saw Jim lean over with the gaff. The improbable had happened – Doodie had caught a salmon!

Jim started up the outboard and came across to us. "It's getting a bit too rough for pleasure. I suggest we go in to Deer Island for lunch. This wind will probably soon die away." By 2.00 p.m. it was blowing harder than ever. Jim decided it would be too uncomfortable to fish. Both the Johns and I agreed. An hour later, far from the wind abating, white clouds of spray were beginning to be whipped off the surface as vicious gust after vicious gust swept down from the mountains. It was blowing straight down the lough. Although the conditions were worsening I knew, slowly steaming straight into the wind, we could safely make it to where we had gone ashore for tea two days previously. It would be a long walk back to the cars, but, I felt, better than staying where we were. I suggested it to my companions. Doodie looked aghast at the idea, whilst John assured us that, if not before, the wind would drop as the sun went down. I was out-voted 5 to 1.

By 4.30 pm the wind was roaring down the valley, there would be no hope of making it to the beach now. The boats would have been swamped within seconds! I suggested, giving a rather feeble laugh as I did so, to indicate I was being funny, that we should collect firewood just in case we were marooned for the night! Jim pooh poohed the idea, as did the cousins. Cynthia and Doodie, looking most unhappy, half- heartedly joined me. When we had gathered quite a pile, John Martin, with the aid of some petrol started a fire, and, with the little tea left from lunch, produced a weak but welcome brew. Far from dropping at dusk, the wind increased to a frightening degree. The whole lough seemed to be blowing away in a huge white cloud of spray.

We were to learn later that a caravan, parked at Nora's house, just took off and landed at least a hundred yards away upside down in a bog! The wind screamed through the stunted oaks that covered most of the island and the whole hut rocked in a most terrifying way. As I gazed across at the mainland, I thought of the grass-fed geese we had specially ordered for dinner than night. As the storms increased in tempo, so more certain I because that it would be someone else who would be enjoying them. The darkness added to our misery. There was no hope of getting off the island before dawn. We could see lights moving up and down along the shore. What we did not know, was that those on the mainland could only see one boat. John and I had pulled ours right up clear of the water and it could not be seen. Further, there were two other boats out that day. The occupants had taken shelter on the far end of the island. They too, had pulled their boats up and, like one of ours, they were not visible.

We knew nothing of the drama that was going on, nor that we had made front page headlines in one of the Dublin evening papers. The gardai were out in force. Supported by visitors from the hotel and a number of locals, they kept an all night vigil, for it was feared that three of the boats had been swamped and the occupants drowned.

Nora's remained open all night, dispensing hot soup, sent over by the hotel and tots of whiskey. Meanwhile we shivered and spent a miserable night in the hut. We tried to sleep, sitting on the hard wooden benches and leaning against the wall. The noise of the wind and bits of branches crashing onto the roof made it impossible. Except for John Martin, he stretched out on the floor and quickly his snoring

142

nearly drowned out the storm!

Around 3.00 a.m., although the wind still howled and whistled around the hut, it was nearly as light as day from the full moon that shone down from a cloudless sky. John and I topped up the tanks of the two outboards; heaped up the firewood we had collected, smothered it with petrol, and with difficulty, set it alight. For a moment I thought the wind was actually going to blow out the burning petrol! However, soon we had a good blaze going. I was told later, it brought nearly as much comfort to those on the shore as it did to us! We boiled the kettle, never had hot water tasted so good!

As dawn began to break, so the wind began to drop. Having spent much time in my youth fishing off and around Lands End with local fishermen, I had quite a bit of experience in handling small boats in heavy seas. Soon I judged it safe to go and told Jim we were off. I'd had enough of Deer Island! He was dubious, but I assured him that if he followed me he'd be alright. We set off with John sitting on the bottom of the boat, in the bow, as ballast, once we were clear of the boulders along the shore. I followed the line of the islands straight down the lough; away past the landing, where people were congregating on the far side. When I judged I had gone far enough to give me the room I wanted I came about, eased the throttle back and headed into the wind, edging all the time towards the landing.

As Cynthia stepped ashore, a guest from the hotel greeted her, a bottle of Scotch in one hand, Irish in the other. He asked if she would like a drink to warm her up. The answer was yes. He suggested she should get a glass out of our picnic basket. I have seldom seen such a look of withering disdain as she silently took the bottle, she didn't seem to worry which, opened her throat and poured. Minutes later Doodie stepped onto the landing. Thunderclouds would have appeared benign compared with the look on her face. Another of the hotel guests, an ardent fisherman, who had stayed up all night to see if he could assist, offered her a bottle. "Will you go fishing again Mrs. Ganly?"

With venom, that I have seldom seen equalled, she replied in the immortal words of Shaw's Eliza Dolittle – "Not bloody likely."

CHAPTER 11

'The Superintendent from Wexford'

Ten days after our return from Ballynahinch, the Kildare Foxhounds were due to meet close to Bryanstown. There weren't many cubbing mornings left and, as I had not been able to get out for even one, I was determined not to miss the opportunity. The first draw was the covert at the end of Bryanstown drive. As I hacked along the road from the meet beside the Master, I felt confident that hounds would find. Tommy had been out earth stopping during the night. To my certain knowledge, there had been three litters of cubs born on the estate. There was not a very big following, thirty at the most. Amongst them was Patrick Ellis, riding a very showy chestnut that he was trying. I was mounted on a powerful heavyweight, a four year old that had come out of Co. Clare, and as far as I knew, had never seen hounds. However, he had settled well and was taking a keen interest in everything going on around him. We reached the wood and the field spread themselves around it.

Cynthia, Patrick and I went and stood along the lane at one end. On a given signal from the Master, Jack Hartigan, the Huntsman, put hounds into cover. Within second one gave tongue, then pandemonium broke out. There seemed to be foxes and hounds in all directions. Suddenly a cub scuttled out of the briars that adjoined the lane, right under my horse, Pluto, before doubling back. I was caught napping for, with no warning at all, Pluto went straight up on his hind legs, depositing me unceremoniously in the lane. Nothing was hurt but my dignity! Pluto stood motionless, ears pricked, listening to hounds, as I re-mounted. My sudden contact with terra firma led to Patrick passing a few remarks, which he seemed to be addressing to the trees, about people who take four year olds out with hounds for the first time and then doze off. I ceased coffee housing with my wife and friend and paid attention.

Quickly a brace of cubs were accounted for, and then all went quiet except for Jack encouraging hounds at the far end of the covert. Tommy arrived on his bicycle and stood talking quietly with Charlie McManus, who had walked down from the house. Finally, both were silent. Several minutes passed, then barely audible, I heard Tommy hiss as he pointed in the direction of the ditch that ran parallel to the lane. To begin with I could see nothing, then I was able to make out a fox slowly creeping along the hedgerow. I put a finger to my lips and both Cynthia and Patrick virtually froze. Once the cub has passed us, Patrick banged his crop against the saddle flap. The cub, if indeed it was one, fled. It looked very mature as it crossed the lane a hundred yards or so beyond us. Patrick and I hollered like mad.

We could hear Jack doubling on his horn as he galloped up the road and turned into the lane. Hounds raced to him, hit the line and sweet music filled the air as they sped away, whilst the two whippers-in rated some of the young entry that were slowly answering to the horn. Drenagh, in spite of her age, was giving Cynthia a hard time. It was all she could do to stop riding over hounds, as they tore up the lane before streaming away across the field to our left, heading towards Laragh. Patrick, Cynthia and I kept slightly right-handed of the line hounds were taking. It seemed almost certain that our quarry would cross the Ryewater. If this happened, since the river had been dredged, there was no way we could reach the far bank short of swimming, except at the bridge away to our right. I was just considering the possibilities when luck seemed to be with us. Our pilot must have been headed, for he turned back in our direction.

Hounds were running at a cracking pace and obstacles were appearing at an almost alarming rate. North Kildare ditches may not be quite as big as those in Meath but being still well overgrown, they provided some exciting moments. Drenagh was in her element, giving every fence feet to spare. Patrick and I riding unknown quantities, were well pleased to be gentlemen and say 'ladies first'! Not a hundred yards from the bridge, for which we'd been heading, hounds crossed the river and immediately swung back left handed heading for a number of Land Commission small holdings. Just as we arrived at the bridge, Jack, the Master and half a dozen of the field came galloping up. Where the remainder had gone to I had no idea and, frankly, was not too concerned as I faced Pluto up to the first of the narrow topped Land Commission banks. For a big horse he was as nimble as a goat, balancing precariously on the top, before launching himself off the other side. Quickly we were back to jumping ditches, as hounds continued to race ahead. Jack's horse baulked at a particularly nasty ditch. As he swung round for another go, Cynthia cut inside and gave him a lead. I landed almost beside him. Jack turned to me.

"This is no cub. If I could get to them I'd stop them".

On we went for another ten to fifteen minutes before hounds eventually checked baying round the entrance to a large unstopped earth. Jack jumped off his sweating and near blown horse and blew "to ground". The Master rode up, scarlet in the face and puffing nearly as much as his horse. Neither appeared to be very fit! I glanced at my watch and, to my horror, saw that it was twenty-five minutes to eleven. I had a most important meeting in Dublin at noon. No way was I going to make it on time, for I estimated we must be at least six miles from Bryanstown, then I would have to change and drive into town. We had just reached the road and I was wondering where I could find a 'phone, when a car came round the corner. It was Charlie. Apparently both he and Tommy were sure that the fox that went away from Bryanstown Wood was an adult. In fact Tommy was certain that it was a vixen that had had her cubs in a scratched out rabbit earth at the back of the farmyard. Knowing I had to be in Dublin by mid-day Charlie had brought the car in search of us. I jumped off Pluto. Cynthia decided to come back with me. Reminding Patrick that he and his mother were coming to dinner that evening I gratefully got into the car and drove off, leaving Charlie to bring the horses home.

George and Maureen McVeagh also joined us that evening. When the ladies had left and we were enjoying our port and cigars, Patrick told us that they had a new sergeant of the Garda Siochana at Straffen and, apparently, he was a right bounder, only that wasn't the word Patrick used! They reared a lot of pheasants on the Straffen House Estate, in fact it was one of the best keepered shoots in the country. In accordance with the law Patrick, as usual, had applied for the required licence to shoot hens. To his amazement and anger, the sergeant had refused, saying he was totally against shooting hens, whether reared or wild. It was not until Patrick threatened to, if necessary, see the Chief of Police, that the Sergeant had issued the required permit. However, since then it seemed that the latter was 'gunning' for anyone or anything to do with the estate. Local gossip had it that the Sergeant had been passed over for promotion and, as a result, was carrying a chip on his shoulder.

The evening drew to a close, George and Maureen left. Molly, Patrick's mother, thanked me for a lovely evening and said, "If we don't meet before, I'll see you on the 8th."

"On the 8th? What's happening then?

"Why, hasn't Patrick said anything? We are hoping you will be able to be with us to shoot pheasants."

Patrick joined in. "No, I hadn't said anything yet. I was keeping it as a farewell surprise! Anyway, it's said now. We'll be moving off sharp on nine o'clock, so don't be late."

I assured him that I wouldn't be and thanked him profusely. Days pheasant shooting in Ireland were a rarity. I had shot at Straffen before. Not only was it an excellent shoot, but they were great fun days as well. John, the gamekeeper, was really a first rate fellow, good at his job, both at rearing and putting birds over the Guns. It was a day to look forward to.

The following morning, I had only just arrived at the office in Dublin when George Ridley telephoned me. He'd been dining with the Duke the night before. The latter had decided to make a present of a top quality heavy weight hunter to a friend who had recently done him a kindness. Like everything else he wanted it yesterday! The instructions had been, 'Tell Twist to drop everything and go and find one.' George also told me that, at the moment, the Duke was planning to come to Ireland in early November. My heart sank. Would this mean that my day's shooting at Straffen would have to be cancelled?

Later that morning I phoned Nat Galway Greer, that great judge of hunters, who had produced so many champions at the Dublin Horse Show. Nat, who had on several occasions in the past, found me horses when I wanted one for the Duke, had nothing to offer. He said he would contact his 'scouts' and see what he could find. In the meantime if I got fixed up, not to worry. I telephoned J.J., he assured me he had the greatest heavyweight in all Ireland. This paragon, apparently, had the manners of a saint, was just 17 hands high and would jump around Aintree if asked. I listened to a five minute eulogy of this equine wonder, which finally finished with an invitation.

"I'm tellin' you, this lad's a Christian. Not a bad thought in his head. Come down on Saturday and ride him cubbing. You'll no leave him once you've thrown a leg across him." I accepted the offer and after a bit more chat rang off. I phoned Cynthia to tell her I'd be away on Friday night, but hoped to be back in time to go to a party we'd been invited to the following evening.

Saturday morning found me astride a magnificent brown gelding.

148

He appeared to be everything J.J had claimed. In fact I could only find one thing wrong with him. When I had him run out, before mounting him, I noted he dished badly with his off fore. Had it not been for that he was a top class show horse. The first draw was Micky's gorse. It was the first time I had been there since the Captain's farewell hunt. We spread ourselves out around the covert. It quickly became apparent that there were at least two cubs on the go. One was soon killed, but a second broke away, taking a line diametrically opposite to that which had supplied so much jumping the last time I had visited Micky's gorse.

Luke now hunted hounds and had been showing great sport. The new Master was very popular, but no huntsman. Fortunately he knew it and after a few abortive attempts, handed the horn over to Luke. Fences loomed up at an almost breath taking speed – mostly banks. My mount jumped with skilful confidence. He was an armchair ride, fast, but didn't pull and obviously enjoyed what he was doing. I was just thinking that I need look no further when I spied a gateway with a number of heavy poles across it. Whilst the rest of the field took on the massive banks either side, I steadied my lad and put him at the timber. He cleared it with consummate ease. I was fortunate in finding three more such obstacles. He sailed over them all without hesitation. J.J. was right. I wouldn't be leaving this fellow. Hounds rolled their quarry over in the open after an invigorating twenty minutes.

I rode over to J.J. who was mounted on his beloved St. Patrick.

"I've seen all I want of this fellow. So, I must get back to Maynooth, I'll call it a day."

J.J. looked at me. "Well?"

"Well what?"

"What do you think of him? Isn't he the greatest yoke you ever threw a leg over?"

"I don't know I'd go as far as that, but he's not bad I'll grant you. He'll probably do. It's a pity he dishes. What are you asking for him?"

"To you, an' I'm telling you it'd be more to anyone else, £500."

"That's great. Now I know what you're asking. The thing is what will you take?"

J.J. gave me a sideways glance.

"Haven't I had enough too. We'll talk business on the way home.

Bid me." I did, less than a third of what he was asking. This led to a withering look and a long spiel on the scarcity of top quality heavyweights. The 'deal' was all part of the spice of life. J.J. would have been really put out if I'd agreed his asking price. So we rode back to his yard, arguing happily over the price, which nevertheless continued to come down. As we turned in at the gate I played my final card.

"Split the difference and it's a deal. It that's not good enough I'm off." After a moment's hesitation J.J. leant towards me.

"You're a terrible hard man, so you are. It's robbed I am, but hold your hand out." I did as I was bid. He smacked his hand hard down on mine. "He's yours and may he be lucky."

We went into the bar and I wrote out a cheque. When he saw it was from one of the Duke's accounts he nearly went into orbit! He assured me that, had he known who I was buying it for, I would not have had the horse for less than the asking price. I didn't spoil John Joseph's day by telling him that, if necessary, I would have paid it! I phoned George Ridley when I returned home and told him I'd bought a horse. Just before he rang off he said. "Oh, by the way, the Duke is crossing on the night of the 8th." I put the phone down with a sigh of relief.

A slight frost glistened on the lawn as I loaded my gun and cartridges into the car. I collected Jill from the kennels and, having said goodbye to Cynthia, I was on my way. She was joining us for lunch and coming out for the afternoon. When I arrived at Straffen, the other guns were there, although there was still fifteen minutes to the off. I knew them all and, having drawn for numbers, we were on our way bang on nine o'clock. According to Patrick I had drawn 'the hot seat' for the first drive. He also told me he was going to do a little juggling with the numbers on the second one as he had a special job for me.

Patrick had been right in his prediction. Birds streamed over me. All in all I felt I acquitted myself reasonably well. When we'd picked-up we walked on towards the second drive. This was a long stretch of woodland bounded by the demesne wall and a road beyond it. It was when we reached the former that Patrick told me what the special job was that he was entrusting to me. He wanted me to walk down the road and stop anything I could from going across to his neighbour. If I remember correctly his name was Houlihan.

"A real thorn in the flesh" as far as the gamekeeper, John, was concerned, for he poached anything he could. Having given me my instructions, Patrick went off to place his guns. When the drive started, one of the beaters was to let me through a door in the wall. I was told there was a similar one about half a mile along the road through which I was to return. I heard a shot, the signal that the drive was to commence. The beater, wishing me luck, let me out onto the road. As Jill and I turned down the side of the wall I heard the bolts slip back into place. I also heard a voice behind me.

"Good morning sorr an' isn't that a great one to be sure." I looked round. It was the sergeant, the one said to be 'a bit of a bounder'. I'm sure I turned several shades paler.

I was still sufficiently English, although I had been in Ireland a number of years, to have immediate feelings of guilt. Even in Ireland it was an offence to shoot on the road. What made it worse was I knew my line of retreat was cut off. There was no chance of going back through the gate. It was securely fastened. My brain raced. Whatever I did I mustn't panic. My mouth had gone dry. I swallowed.

"Good morning sergeant, nice to see you." My voice sounded strange.

"Thank you sorr. Watch out now, begob that was a great cock. My apologies, I'm disturbing you. Bang away now sorr, here comes another."

I took a deep breath, swung on a high hen and dropped it into Houlihan's field. Jill quickly retrieved it. The sergeant reached out and took it from me.

"I'm thinking you'll see better if you walk down the centre of the road. I'll watch out for the traffic." I moved out from the grass verge adjoining the demesne wall. I'd been clinging to it as though it gave me some sort of refuge! I did as the sergeant suggested. He didn't seem to be such a bounder; in fact he appeared to be a most likeable fellow. As we continued on our way I managed to pull some real 'screamers' out of the heavens. These were greatly applauded by the sergeant, to a degree that I almost became embarrassed. Readily he carried everything I shot and there was no doubt in my mind that my friend Patrick had greatly maligned him.

We were nearing the track up to Houlihan's house, when I dropped a lovely right and left of cocks over a high hedge that screened the field from the road. I sent Jill, but she was back in a few minutes

151

with nothing. There was something very odd, for she couldn't have missed two birds lying out in a grass field. I moved over to the hedge, accompanied by the sergeant and found a place where we could see through. There, in the centre of the field was Houlihan holding a brace of pheasants, my pheasants! The sergeant put the birds he was carrying on the grass verge.

"Carry on sorr. I'll catch you up when I've put this boyo straight." So saying he burst through the hedge like an angry bull! I did as I was bid.

The sergeant quickly rejoined me. "The varmint. I'm telling you he'll no do that again in a hurry. I'm sorry for the inconvenience caused sorr an' me not here more than three weeks." I assured the sergeant that there was nothing to be sorry about and that I was most grateful for his help in retrieving the two pheasants. I added that I was sure Mr. Ellis would be equally grateful. We continued on our way down the road, intermittently adding to the sergeant's load. I offered to take some, but he wouldn't hear of it. At last we reached the door back into the demesne. It had been a most fruitful walk and had produced a number of really high sporting birds. The door was open. The sergeant came through and put down his load. Nine in all, mostly cocks. No small weight. It was a cool morning, but I noticed beads of perspiration on the sergeant's brow. I pulled out my pocket flask and offered it to him. He hesitated.

"Go on, it'll do you good after lugging that lot all the way down the road. I'm most appreciative of your help." The sergeant reached out and took the flask.

"Well, if you say it's alright sorr, I'll have a nip, even if I am on duty. Sláinte. 'Tis nice to have met you sorr an' glad I am that I could be of help."

Just as he handed back the flask Patrick and John came up. Both greeted the sergeant and asked how I'd got on. I told them and said how good and helpful the sergeant had been. Patrick picked out a nice brace of birds and handed them to my helper. He seemed duly grateful. Then he saluted me smartly, turned on his heel and disappeared through the door in the wall. Just as he reached the road the patrol car came along, picked up the sergeant and was gone. I turned to my two companions, who were grinning from ear to ear and finally gave way to a near hysterical laughter.

"I don't know what's so funny. He's a damned nice fellow. There's absolutely nothing wrong with him." My remark was greeted with further peals of laughter. I became suspicious.

"What the devil have you two been up to? I'll bet it's something to do with shooting on the road. You might have got me arrested." John wiped tears of laughter from his eyes.

"Begob there was never any fear of that. Wasn't I down the village for a drink the other night an' didn't me friend Jerry, him who's been a garda here for years, come in. We had a jar or two together. Well I tells him we have the Superintendent of the Garda Siochana from Wexford shooting here today, so we had. A big tall dark-haired fellow I says, with one of them golden retriever dogs an' the boss was going to ask him to walk down the road an' try an' stop any birds going over to Houlihans. Jerry comes up last night to tell me that the sergeant was going to wait an' make himself known to the super, him being a bit of a creeper an' lookin' for promotion." With that John was off to organise the next drive. I pooh-poohed John's suggestions, as I walked to my next stand with the rest of the guns. I couldn't really believe the sergeant was as black as he was painted.

It was a great day's sport, a record bag for the shoot. The only thing that had ever so slightly marred the afternoon was that I became very tired of being addressed as 'Superintendent'. As I drove home after tea, passing through the village, who should be standing on the corner but none other that the sergeant. He came smartly to attention and saluted – perhaps John was right after all!

CHAPTER 12

'Didn't I tell you me man would wait.'

It was the last weekend of the month and I had gone down to Banagher with Jim and George. Bobby should have been with us, but called off at the last minute. He was, instead, confined to bed with a bad bout of 'flu. The Shannon had recently flooded and then receded, leaving conditions as near perfect as possible. The three of us shot together on Saturday morning. In the afternoon Jim and George had gone off to the Brosna having first dropped me off beyond the Town Callow. This gave me the whole of the latter to shoot, plus the undercuts of the adjoining red-bog. Snipe were plentiful and I was glad that I had filled both pockets of my shooting coat with cartridges.

At the end of a long since silted-up drain that proved most productive, was an old derelict cottage. The wall at one end had, intact, fallen inwards and rested against the chimney. Some old tarpaulins were draped over this, held in place by a number of stones, obviously taken from the further end of the building that had totally collapsed. Under this precarious structure lived an old man. I never knew his name. Danny and other locals always referred to him as 'Yer man in the cottage.' In spite of the appalling conditions under which he lived he seemed a pleasant enough person, had all his faculties and was always ready for a chat. This afternoon was no exception. He greeted me warmly and had obviously been watching my progress towards his home.

"'Tis terrible quare you are chasing after them poor little bits of snipes. Be the hokey wouldn't you be wantin' a bucket full to make a meal?" I offered him a cigarette and took one myself. After we lit up, we stood chatting for five to ten minutes. I said I must be on my way and wished him luck.

As I walked away he called out. "Have a care now, the heels is about an' terrible wicked he's got." This struck me as being an odd remark, but I gave it little thought. I hadn't gone far from the cottage when I had a pleasing right and left, which Jill retrieved with alacrity. I set off across the main callow that stretched right down to the river, zigzagging as I went, to take in all the wet spots. Every one held snipe, providing some great shooting. I was totally absorbed in what I was doing. About half way to the river my thoughts, which were entirely on snipe, were rudely interrupted by the thunder of hooves directly behind me. I glanced round. There, coming full gallop straight for me, was a very large draught horse. He must have been all of seventeen hands high. The way he was approaching did not give the impression that he was coming to see if I had any sugar for him!

He was about thirty yards away and showing no signs of stopping, when I fired a shot in the air. All this achieved was that he gave a quite terrifying squeal of anger and continued towards me. The second barrel blew a hole in the ground just feet in front of him and an equally short distance from me. He reared up, still squealing, hooves beating the air not feet above my head. One thing that was patently obvious in the course of those terrifying seconds was that nobody had thought to geld this fellow! He wheeled, letting fly with both hind legs as he did so, before galloping off. He missed me, but only fractionally. Jill had tucked in behind my legs and was shaking like a leaf. It was only when I went to reload my gun that I realised I was nearly as bad. 'The Heels', for surely this rogue horse must be what the old man had been warning me about, had withdrawn to about a hundred yards. I started to run as hard as I could towards the road. I had not gone far when I heard squealing and the pounding of hooves behind me.

I was gasping for breath as I turned to face my attacker. This time I did not fire into the air, but blew another hole in the ground just in front of him as he thundered towards me. He swung away, galloped off a few hundred yards and stopped. I again reloaded and headed for the road, but it was a long way away. I was beginning to think I was going to make it without a further attack when I heard again the pounding of hooves on the soft turf coming in my direction. I stopped running turned and, trembling, waited. Again the approach was the same. Direct, teeth bared and that awful squealing. Again I blew a hole in the ground, just in front of his hooves. Again he turned and galloped off. As he slowed, around seventy to eighty yards from me, I gave him a charge of No 8s in the backside and ran like hell.

I didn't even wait to see what effect the shot had had on my attacker. I was scared stiff and literally fell over the gate out onto the road and lay where I had landed. Jill, too, had obviously been shaken by the experience, for she pushed close to me and I could feel her trembling. After a few minutes, still breathing heavily, I got to my feet and looked out across the callow. 'The Heels' had disappeared. He was nowhere in sight. Although there was a good half-hour's daylight left I was too shaken to go on shooting. Not that I would have ventured out onto the Town Callow again. I'd seen all I wanted of that for a while, but there were plenty more good places to try on the opposite side of the road. However, I made my way back over the bridge and up the street to the hotel. I emptied my game bag, gave Jill a towel down and put her in my car. Having changed I lay down on my bed. I felt exhausted. I heard Jim and George return and made my way down to the bar where I knew I would find Danny. He was sitting in his usual corner, a near empty glass in front of him. I ordered him another pint and a brandy for myself.

Danny gave me a quizzical look. "Are you alright? It's terrible pale you're looking."

I told Danny of my experience. As my tale unfolded so a broad grin spread across his weathered countenance. "Begob, an' wasn't I meanin' to tell you about that boyo. Terrible wicked he is so. Three men he's creased an' put in hospital. There's been great talk of shootin' him so there has. I'm telling you no man could put a rope on that bucko, for it'd be certain death so it would."

Danny finished his pint. I ordered him another and asked who owned such a brute of a horse. "Why, himself, yer man in the cottage. Didn't he buy him as a foal off Micky Flynn at the fair four years back? He's run wild on the callows ever since. Jumps like a stag so he does an' goes for miles along the river bank."

I enquired why this equine menace had never been gelded. Danny informed me that there were two reasons. Firstly, his owner said he could not afford the five shillings that the operation would cost, and secondly, no one could catch the colt. I told Danny that, in desperation and a very real fear for my life, I had eventually peppered the backside of 'The Heels' with a dose of No 8s at about seventy yards. Danny grinned.

"Begob, he'd be used to that. Hasn't he more shot in his ass than's in your cartridge bag"?

At that moment my friends appeared. They, it seemed had had a great afternoon's shooting and enquired how I had fared. When I told them of my experience they made light of it and felt the poor horse wasn't as bad as I tried to make out. Danny, however, soon disillusioned them on that score and said that it was only a matter of time before that brute killed someone.

It was early in January when I was next at Banagher. The weather was remarkably mild, more like October than mid winter. There was a good showing of snipe and, quite literally, thousands of golden plover around. Saturday, whilst warm, was windy and I decided to mainly concentrate on the latter. Jim and George, snipe purists that they were, went after their favourite quarry. We all had good shooting, although I should have had more. My reflexes were slower than usual and, to shoot either snipe or goldies, one has to be a hundred percent 'on the ball'.

The plan for Sunday was that we would shoot until lunchtime, making as early a start as possible. Danny and Bill would go to 8.00 a.m. mass, so we should be away from the hotel three quarters of an hour later. Sunday dawned bright and warm, but, alas, that all important factor when snipe shooting, wind, was conspicuous by its absence. I walked out to the bridge with Jill before breakfast and leaned against the parapet. All was peace, the river almost blue in the morning sunlight, whilst a dozen or so curlew flew across the Town Callow, their plaintive cry marking their leisurely progress. The angelus started to ring, summoning the devout to prayer and me to breakfast! Danny and Bill would soon be with us.

Snipe were very plentiful, but, because of the lack of wind, they were getting up, in most cases, several gun shots away. However, a number did sit long enough for us to get within range. Jim and I were shooting well, but George was at his dazzling best! As well as snipe we were getting a nice smattering of teal and, to Danny's delight 'an ole green-neck'. The plan had been to be back at the hotel by 1.00 p.m. for lunch. We finished a very productive walk soon after half twelve. The next one would take at least an hour. Jim and I were all for calling it a day, but George was anxious to continue. After some discussion we came round to George's way of thinking, but Bill looked distinctly worried. I asked him what the trouble was. He explained that he had promised to do a driving job at two o'clock and that by the time we'd finished shooting, returned to the hotel and he'd had his dinner, he was going to be at least an hour late. After a good deal of cajoling by George he finally agreed saying.

"Ah well, me man'll wait. He's all the time in the world so he has."

It was a highly successful walk, in fact the best shooting we had over the weekend, but it was nearly two o'clock before we were back at the Shannon View. The urgency of Bill's driving job seemed to have diminished, for he had a pint with us and we left him and Danny having a second as we went into lunch.

Later, I went outside to pack my gear into the car. The sun beat down and it was really hot. Danny brought the birds out onto the pavement and started to divide them into three equal piles. I glanced up the road, there, heading towards us, was the most dilapidated hearse I had ever seen. The windscreen was starred and almost opaque, the bodywork covered with rust, whilst steam drifted up from the overheated radiator. It was followed by about half a dozen men; a very small number for an Irish funeral.

As the small cortege drew nearer, Danny stood up, crossed himself, and turned to me.

"You know 'your man in the cottage', him as lived on the callow?"

"Yes."

"Well that's him." As the funeral procession drew level, Bill leaned out from behind the steering wheel, gave me a cheery wave and with a broad smile on his face called out. "Didn't I tell you me man'd wait?"

Subsequently we were to hear that there was a sequel to the sad occasion. 'The Heels' was never seen after the day of the funeral. Further, when some men went out to the remains of the old cottage on the Town Callow they turned over a pile of bedding and found a tin box – in it was £680. This was a small fortune in the West of Ireland in those days. Under normal circumstances such a sum would have meant a nice little cottage and the owner being classified as a 'snug man'.

The shooting season was coming to a close and arrangements were made that we would shoot Ballygar the last weekend. Alas, at the eleventh hour, I had to call off, as I was urgently required on the Saturday morning at the stud in Limerick. It was late in the afternoon when I got back to Bryanstown, feeling thoroughly disgruntled. The man I was to have met had missed his flight to Shannon Airport! He was now coming on Monday, so I could have gone shooting. The only consolation was that for virtually the entire way from Bruree it had rained. Walking Island Case, or for that matter any other bog, in such weather would have been little, or no fun. Nevertheless it was the end of the season and it irked that I was missing it.

As Cynthia and I had a pre-dinner drink, sitting in front of a roaring log fire, the rain driving against the window, shooting was uppermost in my mind. Could I arrange something for the morrow? I even thought of going off to Athlone to join my friends, but having already had a long and tiring journey it just did not make sense for half a day. I knew the others were coming home at lunchtime. Just then the phone rang. It was Bobby. Would I join him the following day to shoot in Meath? The answer was a very definite yes.

We met in Dublin soon after eight o'clock and went in Bobby's car. As we drove out of the city along the quays, heading for Phoenix Park, the rain was coming down like the proverbial stair rods. There was not a soul to be seen and I reflected on the wisdom of the inhabitants in remaining indoors on such a morning. Undoubtedly they were right and we were wrong! We were nearing Athboy when Bobby slowed down. We were level with the field where I had first shot a golden plover. It appeared to be devoid of any form of life, certainly there were no plover on it. As we made our way through the town, the rain continued unabated. One of our major problems was going to be keeping our cartridges dry. In those days waterproof cases were still a thing of the future. On really wet days, we used to keep our ammunition in sponge bags, within our jacket pockets; always carried a cartridge extractor and I had a cleaning rod which conveniently unscrewed into three sections, which comfortably fitted into my game bag. Over the years it had removed many a swollen cartridge case after it had been fired.

We pulled up at a gap in a hedge. It led through to the field where the first marsh we intended shooting was situated. I opened the car door; the rain hit me in the face. I closed it again quickly.

"What do you think?" Bobby put his head out, withdrew it hurriedly and wiping the rain off his face said, "Come on, now that we're here, we may as well shoot for a while."

We let the dogs out and set off across the field. I could soon feel the rain soaking through to my shoulders. Waxed waterproof shooting coats were a joy to come! Our shooting garb, at that time, was the same wet or fine. An old tweed jacket, slacks and spiked rubber golf shoes. I, and indeed my friends, had tried various waterproof coats, but found they impeded our shooting and were uncomfortably hot. The great thing on a wet day was to keep going and so one kept warm.

We reached the edge of the marsh; there was a lot of 'fresh'. When there was a marked increase in the water level in a marsh, this normally meant that the snipe would be 'mad wild'. We moved forward as quietly as we could, the rain and what little wind there was in our backs. Usually, this hole was good for a brace or two if one was lucky. On this occasion it did better. What snipe there were sat very tight. Bobby had two right and lefts. I had a single and just as we were finishing the walk, a right and left. The rain was partially forgotten with seven snipe already in the bag. As we approached the gap onto the road, I could see someone standing there. Bobby said it was the owner. If I remember correctly his name was Liam O'Dwyer.

He greeted us warmly. "Good day men an' isn't that a soft morning? Terrible keen you must be chasing them little bits of snipes on a day like this. Are you shooting the bog-hole away up the boreen?" Bobby replied that we were.

"Well, in that case, watch out for an ole cock pheasant. He's just crep in there. If you can bag him, I'd take it kindly if you'd leave him at the cottage so I would. Good luck men, I must away to mass." With that he got on his bike and rode off towards the village.

The bog hole added a further four snipe and a teal. The latter was flying over and Bobby pulled off a really spectacular shot. As he said, one that made it worthwhile getting drenched to the skin. There was no sign of the pheasant in the marsh. We made our way back towards the car, hugging the hedges for shelter. Jill, who was at my heel, suddenly stopped. Obviously she had winded something. Bobby nipped smartly back to a gap we had just passed and I told Jill to 'get in'. Almost immediately I heard a pheasant rise on the far side of the hedge. The next thing Bobby fired. Fractionally later I heard him send his labrador bitch, Bella. Apparently he hadn't a clear view and only winged 'the ole cock'. By the time I joined Bobby, Bella had disappeared over the brow of the hill. We had to wait several minutes before she reappeared bearing the pheasant. Certainly Liam had been right about it being old. I have seldom seen longer spurs; they must have been nearly an inch! We made our way to the cottage and knocked on the door.

Mrs. O'Dwyer opened it. I explained our presence and Bobby handed over the pheasant. "My, but himself will be that pleased. Isn't it four years or more he's been after that boyo. Come in, men, for a cup. I have the tay brewed."

We accepted gratefully. Pools of water appeared on the flagged floor as we drip-dried. The tea was black, sweet and so strong one could nearly have stood a spoon up in it, but oh, so beautifully hot! The smoke from the turf fire stung my eyes, but compared with outside, it was bliss. After about a quarter of an hour, with some reluctance, at least on my part, we left the shelter of the cottage. The rain continued, but it seemed to be easing. Still the snipe sat tight as we went from marsh to marsh. Seldom, if ever, have I known snipe sit like it. By the time we stopped for lunch we had shot nearly thirty. Our sandwiches and soup did not take long; it was no day for a picnic! We didn't even bother to sit in the car. We drained better standing up!

Soon we were on our way again. However, for some inexplicable reason the snipe suddenly had become 'mad wild', getting up two gunshots away and screeching off into the distance. Nevertheless, we managed to come within range of sufficient to keep adding to the bag, even if not at the rate we had achieved in the morning.

We were nearing the bottom of a hill that had more twists in it than a corkscrew, when I asked Bobby to pull in on the grass verge opposite an old tumbled down cottage. He did as I requested, but at the same time asking why? I explained that, over the brow of the hill, out of sight of the road, was a marsh. He was a bit sceptical, for he thought he knew every bit of bog and wet place in Co. Meath. However, I assured him that I had shot it earlier in the year with another of our friends, Tim Walker.

Our path took us past the cottage and I noticed that a small section of the roof was still intact. The floor beneath it was dry. As we breasted the hill and looked down on the bog, the wind was noticeably stronger and it was getting colder by the minute. My choice for our last walk of the day proved to be a good one. Snipe were plentiful, if wild, and we added some weight to the bag with a brace of mallard and three teal. As we returned to the car the rain, which had kept off for most of the afternoon, came down harder than ever. Bobby remarked that the sooner we were out of our saturated clothes the better. I fully agreed.

I nonchalantly put my gun in the car, grabbed my holdall with my dry clothes and made a run for the cottage. My friends' language was, to put it mildly, explicit. He too had noticed that one sheltered spot and, like me, had said nothing. There wasn't room for the two of us and it had become too cold to hang around in wet clothes. Bobby, still muttering, laid his dry things out in the back of the car and, leaving the door open, came across the road into the shelter of the cottage wall to strip off.

This he quickly achieved and was on his way back to the car, when round the corner, free wheeling happily on her bike, came a lady of ample proportions. She saw Bobby. The peace of the countryside was shattered by a piercing scream. She wobbled frantically for about fifteen yards, before going virtually head first into the ditch. Bobby, with great presence of mind, continued his dash to the car, wrapped his towel around himself and ran down the road to her rescue. Fortunately I was still partially in my sodden clothes and quickly joined him. Bobby enquired.

"Are you alright mother? Haven't you ever seen a naked man before?"

"Begob, I have that sorr, plenty of times, but never racing at me from the bushes like a maddened banshee. Holy Mother of God, didn't you put the heart crossways in me?"

Bobby led her back up to the car, whilst I collected her ancient bicycle and straightened the handlebars. Bobby found his wallet, extracted a note and gave it to 'herself'. It was received with enthusiasm. "God bless you sorr and thank you. An' isn't it the great body you have." With that she was on her bike with a speed and lightness of foot that belied her weight. With a cheery wave she was gone.

It was just three o'clock when we stopped in Athboy for tea; barmbrack and a large Powers. It had been a memorable day from several aspects, of which by no means least was the bag – thirty-seven snipe, two mallard, four teal and 'the ole cock'. In spite of the weather it had been a tremendous end to the season. As we set out for home warm and content, the rain was still coming down like stair rods! A few miles out of Dublin near Clonee, there was a small stretch of road that was regularly subject to flooding. This evening was no exception, but on this occasion there was a difference. Stuck, two thirds of the way across the road, was a large limousine. It appeared that 'stuck' was the operative word. Bobby pulled up and surveyed the situation. He hooted loudly on the car horn. After several blasts, a gauntleted arm appeared waving us on. To pass the stranded vehicle meant that we would have to be tight into the right hand bank, the cause of the flooding and where the deepest water lay. Cursing, Bobby revved up and had a go. I thought we were going to make it, but a length past the car we spluttered to a halt. We looked at each other. There was only one thing to do.

Off came the shoes and socks, we rolled up our trouser legs, climbed out and pushed. As we made it to dry land, we heard a voice calling behind us. A chauffeur was leaning out of the stationary car.

"His Excellency says I'm to tell you to push us out."

I called back. "You both get out and paddle and we'll help you." At that, a rear window was wound down. A very black face appeared. The owner made a grave error in demanding that we should push his car clear of the floodwater. Bobby's reply would, in this day and age, have definitely been described as racist! We got back into the car. Fortunately it started at about the third attempt. As we drove back into town I wondered how long his Excellency would wait before getting his feet wet.

CHAPTER 13

'Held together by paint and providence'

February brought the worst weather of the winter, to be followed by a cold bleak spring. Whilst this did not affect my shooting, for the season now ended for everything on 31st January, it greatly curtailed what few days hunting I might have managed. The raw cold continued into April. Grass, which by the middle of the month should have been reasonably plentiful, was at a premium. Cattle prices dropped, as farmers finished their winter fodder and had to sell or let their stock starve. I received a phone call from my friend Sean Rafferty. Could I help him out and take twenty of the best white-head bullocks a man ever saw? When next I went to Lismore, I called to see Sean, bought his cattle, shipped them over to the Duke's stud farm in England. Out of bad often comes some good, even if only for a few.

The harsh conditions meant that the Mayfly were late hatching on Corrib that year. The Dublin Spring Show was over before this happened. As soon as I heard 'the fly were up' I contacted Peter and arranged for three days' fishing at the end of the week. Peter had recently married and had bought two old cottages that he was busily converting into a guesthouse. He told me that, for the present, he was not working as a gillie, but would take a break from his labours to accompany me. Cynthia, alas, was unable to go with me as she had a prior commitment to judge at a dog show.

I arrived at Oughterard full of hopeful anticipation. Peter joined me at the hotel. For once he was not his usual ebullient self, in fact as he walked into the bar he looked positively dejected. I enquired what the trouble was. Apparently he had been waiting for a friend to come and help him wire the guesthouse and fix the plumbing for over a month. The latter had called earlier in the day to say he would start the job the next day! Peter explained that he had to be there and had spent several hours that afternoon trying to find me a gillie. It was the height of the season and the only person he could get was a young lad who lived a couple of miles up towards the head of the lough. Paddy somebody, I forget his surname. Peter said he should be in any minute to meet me and that as far as he knew he was a reliable youngster, although he did not know very much about him. We had just finished our drinks, when

Paddy arrived. He seemed a pleasant enough lad, although very shy, but alas he hadn't an outboard motor. Peter said I could borrow his. I arranged to meet Paddy around nine o'clock at the cove where he kept his boat and that he should obtain a supply of Mayfly. After a quick drink he left us, leaving Peter and me to gossip. However, the ties of matrimony were strong and he left when I went in for dinner.

The next morning I met Paddy as arranged. The day looked promising, cloudy and just enough wind blowing from the west to produce a gentle wave, ideal for dapping. We loaded the boat, having put two rods up and pushed off. I was about to start the engine when Paddy, hesitatingly suggested that we should do a drift along the shore and round into Boozers Bay. That, strangely enough, was the name of the bay at the mouth of the Oughterard River. Used to going six or seven miles with Peter before we began fishing I couldn't believe my ears. Boozer's Bay was aptly named. There are fishermen and fishermen – those who are there to fish and those who are there for the 'craic'. The latter stayed up most of the night drinking, telling of the ones that got away and appeared when the morning was half over. They would struggle forth and, well supplied with their favourite tipple, drift idly around in the bay until they felt it was time to return to the bar! This resulted in the trout in Boozer's Bay and the surrounding shallows being well versed with every type of lure available! Peter once said he thought the trout in that area, at the height of the dap, must have about twenty chances a day to give themselves up!

I turned to Paddy. "Let me make on thing clear, I'm here to fish. I know and you should know that the chances of doing this successfully around the mouth of the river are virtually nil. Do you or do you not know the lough?"

"I do that sorr. Wasn't me granda one of the greatest fishermen ever to set foot on it." I let the latter comment pass, although it did suggest that Paddy had biblical connections! "Right, we'll go across to the far side. I've always done well around the islands over there with Peter."

Paddy smiled. "You're the boss." I started up the engine and set off. Half an hour later we were gently drifting down the back of an island, but there was little activity. Paddy caught a 'tiddler' that was immediately returned; otherwise we never saw a sign of a trout. We finished the drift, I started up the motor and we moved on about a quarter of a mile to the next lot of shallows. These extended for the better part of a mile, a favourite place of Peter's and where, over the years, I had landed some good fish. The sun kept breaking through, as the wind grew stronger and the wave increased. The blow-lines billowed out, like spinnakers on a yacht, as the Mayflies on our hooks danced and skittered on the waves. There is quite an art in keeping the flies on the water. One's bait has to look like a freshly hatched fly about to take off. A number of mayfly were floating all around us, obviously there was a good hatch.

Suddenly I saw a trout rise slightly to the right of our drift. Seconds later it rose again, it certainly was not a run of the mill two to two and a half pounder. It was big. Not one of the monsters from the deep, but surely four to five pounds. I asked Paddy to ease the boat in towards the shore so that we would drift over the place I had seen the big fish rise. There it was again. The adrenaline flowed as my fly danced and jigged on the waves, drawing ever nearer. Suddenly, with a mighty splash caused by a classic head and tail rise, my lure disappeared. I waited a second and struck. The rod bent double, the line screamed off the reel. Paddy, grinning from ear to ear, started to reel in. Bang, he hooked a fish too, within feet of the boat. Wisely he held the line firm, risking losing the trout as he scooped it in with the net. It was a keepable size. Hastily he got on the oars and started to follow the line that went singing through the water.

Twice, in quick succession the trout jumped. "Begob he's a monster, don't lose him sorr." Paddy rowed harder in the wake of the powering trout. I had no intention of losing such a fish, at least not if I could possibly avoid it. Suddenly it turned and headed straight for the boat. Fortunately Paddy was 'right on the ball' and backwatered frantically. I could plainly see the big trout as it shot across the bows of the boat only feet below the surface. But for Paddy's quick thinking I could well have lost it. The fight continued for another ten minutes or so, then I got the upper hand. Paddy skilfully manoeuvred the net and my prize was in the boat. Quickly dispatched, I took out my spring balance and weighed it – six and three quarter pounds. The biggest brown trout I had ever caught on the dap and, as it turned out, ever would.

I could see trout rising all around us and without more ado we were back fishing. The cloud had cleared and the sun shone brightly, too brightly, for whilst trout kept rising to our flies, they had started to come short, bumping rather than taking our bait. However, some still came at the flies and meant it. I had another lovely fish that turned the scales at just over three and a half pounds. Around 1.30 p.m. all went quiet and when we had not seen a trout move for half an hour, I decided it was time for lunch. Paddy rowed the boat in to a nearby island, built a fire and made the tea. He then went off to sit on his own. I told him not to be so silly and stay with me. Once we'd exhausted the 'big feller' as a topic of conversation, getting Paddy to talk was hard work. However, I learned that he was the eldest of a family of nine and that his 'ma' was 'expecting'. I also discovered that his ambition, as soon as he was eighteen was to go to England to join the Navy. For something to say, I enquired about his boat. He told me that he'd had it new the previous autumn. I looked at it and thought that if that was the case then he'd not looked after it very well.

When we pulled out from the island to resume fishing, it was obvious that the wind had increased considerably. So much so that it was hard to keep the flies on the water. There was not a lot of activity. Paddy lost a good fish and I added one or two more keepable ones to the bag. Around tea time it had become so rough that I decided to head for home. In the shelter of an island I filled up the petrol tank, whilst Paddy took down the rods. When this was done, I started up the motor and we set out across the lough. As soon as we were clear of the island and the shelter of the mainland I realised how rough it had become. It was going to be a wet trip! What made it worse was that our course was diagonally across the waves; making the boat bounce and yaw in quite an alarming manner. I glanced at Paddy, who I had told to sit on the forward thwart and bail when necessary. He looked positively terrified as he clung to the seat with both hands. An extra big wave landed a dollop of water in his lap.

He turned almost green as he shouted back at me. "Jasus, we'll be drounded. We should have stayed on the island."

"Nonsense." I cut the engine back as far as I dared. "We'll take it slowly. This is nothing a good strong boat can't take. Now bail, that is unless you want the boat to sink." My last remark seemed to galvanise Paddy into life and, crossing himself, he set to work with a vengeance. By the time we were halfway across the wind was really gusting down from the mountains. At one stage I did consider heading back into the wind for the nearest island. However, having been on Corrib several times with Peter when conditions were worse I kept going. Half an hour later we were back. As I beached the boat I looked at Paddy. His hands were clasped, his eyes tight shut, his lips moving. I said nothing.

After a few minutes Paddy stood up. He looked pale and shaken.

"Jasus, that was terrible. 'Tis the first time I've been across an' I'm telling you it'll be the last."

"I thought you said you knew Corrib well?"

"I does that, just around here, but I've never been that far from the shore before."

I said nothing, there wasn't really much to say!

Paddy helped me load my rods and tackle into the car and carried the fish up. Nine beautiful trout, easily the best day I ever had on Corrib. They averaged just over two and a half pounds. Before I left I asked Paddy if he'd be up at the hotel later in the evening. He assured me he would. Peter joined me around seven, not a happy man. The plumber/electrician had not turned up, but had promised to be there the next day. Peter admired my catch, particularly the 'big feller'. Hotel guests had caught only one or two other trout. Apparently because of the wind they hadn't got much further than the bay. Paddy arrived later, had a drop of the 'hard stuff' to celebrate our day, followed by a couple of pints of porter. By the time he left he was all for going back across the lough next day!

It was bright and still when I joined him the following morning. As we pulled the boat down into the water, I could see little hope of equalling the previous day's catch. I climbed aboard and Paddy poled the boat back with an oar. The engine fired first pull. I put the tiller over to head out across the lough and went to sit down. As I did so I glanced down at the bottom of the boat. There was at least six inches of water in it and rising fast! I brought the boat about as quickly as possible, opened up the throttle and ran it up onto the beach.

"What the devil's wrong Paddy? Have you had the bung out and forgotten to put it back?"

"I has not. I'm thinking she has a class of a leak so she has."

"You can say that again." We pulled the boat out of the water, unloaded it and turned it over. The cause of the leak was immediately obvious; both planks either side of the keel had sprung. Daylight was clearly visible through the cracks. "I though you said this was a new boat last autumn?"

"That's right, new to me. She were built for my granda a good thirty five years ago."

It was my turn to say "Jasus". We'd come right across the lough, in really rough weather, in something held together by paint and providence! As I thought of what might easily have happened I turned cold. No wonder Paddy had never ventured far from the shore before and had prayed most of the way home! I could only thank God that his prayers had been answered. I gave him a stern but quiet lecture and told him that, even when fixed, he should not venture across the lough again in his 'new' boat. He assured me that he wouldn't and that he had already ordered a truly new boat from the builders in Galway. A sixteen footer and it would cost £2 per foot.

That was the end of my three days' fishing. I paid Paddy, wished him well and went off to see Peter. He was shattered by what I told him and I am sure genuine when he said he had no idea that Paddy was so stupid, or his boat so ancient. I phoned Cynthia to tell her I'd be home by teatime and to suggest that she contact four of our closest friends to come and dine on Corrib trout. They are wonderful eating and have firm pink flesh, rather like salmon. Peter always claimed that this was because they lived largely on freshwater shrimps.

The summer passed rapidly. In August Willy Ganly was in London and came back with lightweight canvas waders, ideal for snipe shooting. We all immediately invested in one or two pairs, except George. He said that we were getting soft and would not be able to walk any great distance in them. He was wrong. Waterproofed shooting jackets were also becoming the 'in thing'. It looked as though the spartan days of snipe shooting were nearly over!

One thing that was becoming alarmingly obvious was that the government's land drainage scheme was beginning to have an adverse effect on the snipe population. Whilst we still had good shooting around Meath in the early part of the season, there was not the number of homebred snipe to be seen as in years gone by. The quantity of migratory ones seemed to be on the decline too, particularly on the red-bogs around Ballygar. No longer were big bags a certainty. Whereas, in the past one could be sure there would be snipe in large quantities, now this was a variable feature of our sport. In spite of this we still had some wonderful days and always hoped that things would return to what they had been.

It was early in December that Jim, George and I arrived at Banagher one Friday night. Danny was waiting in the bar. He looked positively excited. "Begob men, you should have your food an' be away out after the geese. There's thousands of them an' the moon is right. I'm telling you the Town Callow is alive with them so it is." Danny was surprisingly persistent, but we held firm. We were there to shoot snipe and duck and, of course, golden plover. None of us had a desire to sit out on the callows half the night. When we'd had our meal, we returned to the bar and settled down for 'a bit of gas' – plenty of chat and leg pulling with the locals, many of whose land we shot over. We plied them with drink, but always remained abstemious ourselves. Around ten o'clock Jim and George headed for bed whilst I took Jill for a last walk. I turned right out of the hotel and headed on over the bridge, stopping at the gate leading into the Town Callow. The one I had fallen over the afternoon I had met 'The Heels'.

The moon was up, it was nearly full. From the cackling and honking rising from over the callow it did not seem that Danny had in any way exaggerated. As I stood in the shadows listening, a skein glided in, quietly honking, not twenty yards over my head. It was only a matter of minutes before there was another lot and then another. I was momentarily tempted to go back for my gun, but resisted. Instead I spent a fascinating hour or so watching and listening. Although it was hard to tell for sure, it seemed that the majority were White fronted with a lesser number of greylag. widgeon, teal and pintail were flying the line of the river, as were curlew and green plover. There was a cacophony of sound and there is no knowing how long I might have remained had not Jill made it clear that, if there wasn't going to be any action, we might well go back to bed. Next morning over breakfast I told my friends about my walk. George – a snipe purist – one could hardly persuade him to remain in a hide for a morning duck flight – made a great thing about my not having called them. Jim, however, quite rightly pointed out that one shot and the geese would have been gone. They had thousands of acres on which to feed.

The morning's sport was good, but nothing special and we had to work hard for what snipe we did get. Jim, quite unintentionally, shot a Great Snipe. One of the only three that I knowingly saw during the twenty-three years I was in Ireland. After lunch Jim and George headed off for the Brosna, having first dropped me out beyond the Town Callow. Bill was to come back for me later. My walk was much the same as the memorable one when I had met 'The Heels'. I started along the undercuts of the red-bog – areas where the turf had been cleared and rushes started to grow. I walked for about half a mile and never saw a snipe. I decided to take a turn out onto the bog, but I wasn't very hopeful. I had covered less than a hundred yards when suddenly, exploding into chattering flight, a grouse rose from almost under my feet. I was so surprised that I missed it completely with the first barrel, but was spot-on with the second; truly a red-letter day. It was in great condition, a young bird and was the only grouse I saw round Banagher in all the years I shot there.

I had added a few snipe and a couple of golden plover to the bag by the time I joined Bill. It had been an interesting walk; in so far that I had seen a large number of geese, but none had come within many hundred yards of me. Bill drove me to the far end of the Brosna Callow and parked by a cottage. I could see Jim and George away in the distance, Danny walking between them. I went off to shoot several small marshy holes. Snipe were scarce, but I did shoot a right and a left, really the only chance I had. Jim and Danny arrived back at the car a few minutes after me. Jim, too, had found birds to be very few and far between. The light was going rapidly, but George, ever keen, was exploring every wet spot. About two hundred yards from where we stood, was a patch of gorse. In the middle was a marshy area, which was seldom without several snipe. George disappeared from sight. Almost immediately a goose rose, just clearing the gorse, flying low and in no apparent haste. A shot rang out and it collapsed. Five minutes later George joined us carrying a huge Greylag – or was it?

He dropped it on the ground in front of us and smiled happily. "There you are Danny, you wanted us to shoot geese. I've shot one for you." Danny looked troubled.

"Be the hokey you have so. Isn't that the widow Mulligan's old gander an' a terrible fierce woman she is too." Before anyone could utter another word, there was a shriek from the cottage door behind us. We turned as one. There stood a portly woman – the Widow Mulligan. She advanced; the look on her face did nothing to belie Danny's assessment. She stopped in front of us hands on hips. "Holy

Mother o' God, isn't it me fine gander you've destroyed. You heathen crature!" She shook her fist in George's face. "An' him hatched the day my Liam was took. Twenty-five years ago it was. It's the law I'll be havin' after you, ...you – you red faced divil!"

At least she was right about one thing – the colour of George's face! She burst into tears.

Danny stepped forward and put a hand on her shoulder. "Ah now mother, don't take on so, it's not that bad. Isn't Mr. Mac a dacent man an' he'll pay you well, so he will."

The tears stopped. "Begob he will that. Me fine goose gone forever." George, always carried a roll of notes, put his hand in his hip pocket. He peeled off two £1 notes watched by the widow. He stopped. The tears started again. He pulled off another. They stopped. George was about to put the remaining notes back in his pocket when the widow was positively convulsed by a heart-rending sob. George reluctantly added two more, before returning the remainder to his pocket with a very definite air of finality. He handed the notes to the Widow.

She beamed. "My, but aren't you the great gentleman an' wasn't it time the ole creature was deaded anyways?" George went to lift the gander into the car. The Widow drew herself up, eyes flashing. "An' where dose you think you're taking me fine bird? Wasn't it the shooting of the crature you paid for not the meat." With that she whipped up the goose and marched back into the cottage slamming the door. There was silence and then we all broke into uncontrollable laughter, except George. He just didn't seem to be able to see what was so funny.

CHAPTER 14

'The last big bag of snipe on the Shannon'

The years passed quickly. Agricultural 'progress' reached the Emerald Isle. The leisurely life in the country changed rapidly. In many areas, where once relaxed and convivial hours were spent delivering milk to the creameries, now lonely minutes served taking the churns out to the roadside, from where they would be collected by lorry. Tractors took the place of horses and, still a novelty, combine harvesters began to make their appearance. The value of land was beginning to be appreciated and rising in price at an alarming rate. This in turn led to widespread drainage. It wasn't just ditches being cleared and marshy fields drained. Rivers were dredged. Whole areas that had been the natural habitat of snipe and duck disappeared to be replaced by a wealth of arable land and lush pastures,

However, this was not all that confronted the wildfowl in their fight for existence. The Irish Tourist Board, in their quite proper efforts to improve the economy, gave much prominence to the country's wonderful fishing and shooting. Suddenly it seemed that parties of would-be sportsmen were arriving every week. It wasn't, at least to begin with, what they shot, the trouble was what they disturbed. This, coupled with the fact that many more residents were taking up wildfowling, meant that marshes and bogs shot five or six times in a season at the most in past years were now being disturbed two, sometimes three times a week. The interest in snipe, certainly by the Irish wildfowlers, was negligible, but, alas, snipe do not like being continually chivvied and harassed.

In spite of this we still walked the countryside for hours, loving every minute of it and ever hopeful. Sometimes we would be amply rewarded, others not. It truly became a case of 'you never can tell'. There were days when it seemed that nothing had changed. One such day was the 22nd October 1960.

David and Bobby Ganly and I met Mount (The Earl of Mount Charles) early one morning in Kinnegad, on our way to Banagher to shoot snipe. Danny had phoned to say that the like of the snipe had never been seen before. Bobby quickly joined our guest in his car and we were on our way. I knew Mount quite well, had judged Field Trials with him and had once shot pheasants at a shoot where he was a guest. He was a noted pheasant shot, but I had no idea how he would perform at snipe. Not infrequently, guns who are brilliant at high overhead birds, are lost when it comes to shooting something flying away from them, particularly when it jinks and swerves as do departing snipe. We pulled up outside The Shannon View just as dawn was breaking. Even in the poor light, I thought Mount had a distinctly jaundiced look about him. As they say in Ireland, he did not look in the whole of his health! I was right. It transpired that he had been up most of the night consoling a friend whose wife had left him. Consolation, amongst other things, apparently, had been derived from a bottle or two of vintage port!

Bobby, David and I went up to an empty bedroom to change into our bog-trotting clothes. Mount said that he was already suitably attired. When we came downstairs we found him, nearly asleep, at a table in the dining room. Rose followed us in with a tray bearing four plates heaped with fried eggs, bacon, black pudding and fried potato. She put one down in front of Mount. He turned several shades paler and pushed it away and asked Rose to fetch him a pint of Guinness. Bobby divided the unwanted helping between the other three plates!

David and I, who were shooting together, were soon ready for the off. Mount, contrary to the advice offered by all three of us, insisted on wearing waders. This led to David turning to me and saying that we'd better get going because, from the way Mount attacked his pint and was now going to don waders, it would be up to us to shoot any snipe that we took home. This led to a quick rejoinder from our friend and the suggestion of a bet of a fiver a corner on who would shoot the most snipe by lunch time. David and I, without hesitation, took up this offer. The handicapping was all in our favour! We were sure we were on a 'cert'.

David and I were to shoot the Brosna Callows. Danny and Bill were going with Bobby and Mount. Not having a driver would mean that we had to walk some of our territory into the wind, but there was so little that it was really of no consequence. Having decided on our plan of campaign we spaced ourselves out and moved forward. We hadn't gone more than forty or fifty yards when, suddenly, the air was full of snipe. I downed a right and left, as did David, but he went one better than me, for he had two with his second barrel. Snipe seemed to be rising everywhere, but with virtually no wind, they were very wild, getting up to a hundred to a hundred and fifty yards ahead. Over the thirteen years I had been in Ireland, I had seen a lot of snipe along by the Brosna, but nothing comparable to what there was that morning. Fortunately, a small percentage sat tight, but it was infuriating to see the numbers that went screeching off well out of range every time we fired. Had there been a wind there is no knowing how many we might have shot. It was an exciting morning and David and I were agreed, that at a most conservative estimate we must have seen something in excess of six hundred snipe. It was, therefore, disappointing that when we returned to the car to go for lunch the count was only thirty-seven for we had both shot well. However, we were confident that we had done enough to comfortably win the wager.

We did not waste time when we got back to the hotel and were halfway through lunch when the others returned. Danny looked round the door. "Well men?"

"A great morning," I replied. "Never seen so many snipe."

"We'll buy you an extra pint out of our winnings," added David. "We shot thirty seven."

A broad grin spread across Danny's face. "Begob, yer bate, so you are. Didn't Mr Bobby an' himself shoot thirty eight and an ole green-neck. I'm telling you your man's like a Jack Snipe so he is, boots an' all." At that moment the others entered and confirmed Danny's report. We paid up willingly, for seventy-five snipe in a morning was no small achievement, whatever the conditions.

Mount had definitely recovered and attacked his lunch with gusto. As soon as he had finished, he rushed up the street to buy a pair of cheap shoes – he'd had enough of waders! Bobby agreed with us and said that, in all the years he had shot at Banagher, he'd never seen so many snipe. As we waited for Mount, we made plans for the afternoon. David had an important meeting in Dublin that evening so our time was limited. We had to be away by 4.00 p.m. at the latest. It was agreed that David and I would shoot, where we liked, across the bridge; which really meant in the time available the Town Callow. Bobby and Mount would stay on the Banagher side of the river. Danny said he'd come with us.

We were about to leave the hotel; the others had already gone, when Danny enquired.

"Did you ever shoot the little hole at the back of the town?"

179

He looked at David. "No, can't say I have, in fact I didn't know there was one there." "There is, an' I'm thinking it'll be alive with snipes." Much discussion then ensued as how best to shoot it. Finally it was decided that David would enter it from the hotel garden, or to be more accurate, where the garden would be if the ground was cultivated. I was to go and stand on the end of the station platform, to shoot anything going forward! I must have looked a bit uncertain at this suggestion, for Danny, grinning from ear to ear, cut in. "Be the hokey don't be worryin' yourself. There'll be no train coming an' won't you be keeping your feet dry?"

I walked down the street the eighty or so yards to the station, Drake, my golden retriever at my heel. I no longer had my beloved Jill. I walked along the platform and took up my position. I felt most conspicuous! I saw David climbing over the fence at the end of the 'garden' and observed Rose hanging out of a back bedroom window, the better to watch the sport. David entered the marsh. The whole area became alive with snipe; they appeared to be going in all directions, but plenty came hurtling out towards me. I kept pushing cartridges into my gun and firing as fast as I could. In a couple of minutes it was all over. I had downed five. I sent Drake to retrieve them. Four were dead, but one gave him a lot of trouble and proved to be a strong runner on the 'up-line'! It is surprising how fast and far a snipe can run. David joined me, he had added four to the bag.

We crossed the bridge and made our way out onto the Town Callow. If we thought we had seen a multitude of snipe in the morning it was nothing to what we saw in the afternoon. They were, however, still unbelievably wild. Only in one place, for no explicable reason, did they 'sit' and here we shot nine without moving our feet. We were back at the hotel just before four o'clock; Bobby and Mount were already there. The bag was 131 snipe, 1 mallard and 2 golden plover.

I may be wrong, but I would say with some certainty, that it was the last sizeable bag of snipe shot around the Banagher area. The big freeze that followed later that year, starting on Boxing Day and carrying on well into 1961, decimated the snipe population. As we climbed into our cars to head for home, Danny, his face flushed from porter and unbridled elation, called out from the doorway. "Good luck now, I'm telling you men, you'll be a long time dead, so you will, afore you see as many snipes again!"

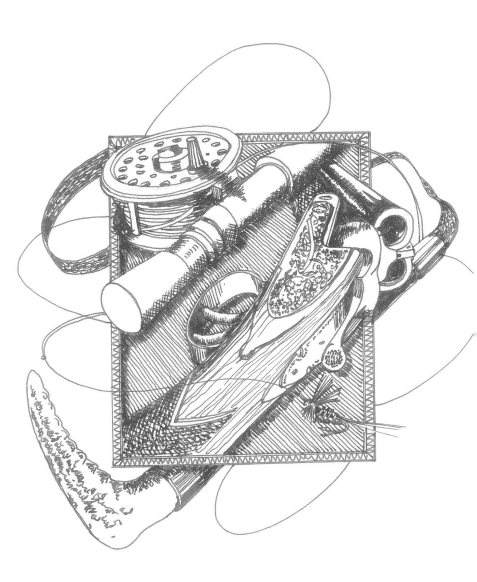

EPILOGUE

Ireland is indeed the "land of Saints and Scholars" but it also breeds true sportsmen of talent and diversity.

As I write this, Michael Twist, now in his 87th year, entered the field he has so aptly described, shortly after the end of the Second World War, and within a trice was up there with the best of them, accepted and loved by those with whom he shared his passionate love of Field Sports.

Only a "Sassenach" could write with such clarity and humour and I was fortunate to have taken part in some of these snipe days with the likes of George McVeagh, the Ganly brothers and Michael and Mervyn Walker, experts of their time and each with individual style. You almost had to run to keep up with George, yet he seemed never to be caught on the wrong foot. I have seen Jim Ganly shoot 20 snipe straight with ne'er a miss, and Mervyn Walker shot with a sawn-off gun with a large back collar stud as a sight with which he would blot out the bird. It worked!

The astonishing number of snipe, before land reclamation and drainage destroyed much of their habitat, made it possible for enthusiasts to establish a profitable snipe round or two within easy reach of home. A bag of 50 snipe between four guns was not uncommon and there were the red-letter days well in excess of this, with the addition of Duck, Teal, Golden Plover and the occasional Goose.

Of course, it did not always turn up trumps and I recall asking a man stacking turf whether I could shoot the red bog, the moon being full. Given the go-ahead, I asked if the snipe were in. The reply "Snipes surr, if yer hadn't yer gun, they'd ate yer."
I walked for more than an hour with not a snipe to be seen.

From Michael I learnt a lot of the finer points of dog handling and judging at a Field Trial. A snipe trial at Banagher was an exacting test, but I doubt that numbers would
be sufficient nowadays.

I count myself privileged to know Michael and commend this delightful book to the
sporting public.

Conyngham